ANUNNAKI PRAYERS
THE CUNEIFORM ALMANAC
NEW STANDARD ZUIST EDITION

POCKET EDITION

Published from
Mardukite Borsippa HQ, San Luis Valley, Colorado
Founding Church of Mardukite Zuism,
Mardukite Academy & Systemology Society
for religious and educational purposes only.

ANUNNAKI PRAYERS

THE CUNEIFORM ALMANAC

NEW STANDARD ZUIST EDITION

Developed by Joshua Free for the
Church of Mardukite Zuism

THE JOSHUA FREE IMPRINT
JFI PUBLICATIONS

A special pocket prayerbook
devotional companion
containing prayers, invocations and
hymns from the cuneiform-tablets
edited for founding the
Church of Mardukite Zuism

Pocket Paperback Edition — *February 2024*

Project Director: Joshua Free
Project Assistant: Kyra Kaos

Some portions of this work appeared previously as
"The Complete Book of Marduk by Nabu"

mardukite.com

The <u>Original</u> Spiritual & Religious Prayerbook on Planet Earth

Ancient Mesopotamian magic and Babylonian mysticism is based on prayers and incantations found today on the surviving cuneiform tablets we have unearthed from the sands of time.

This pocket paperback expanded edition of our Anunnaki devotional companion reveals the original methods of spiritual practitioners to establish a relationship with divinity.

Even if you think you already know all about Ancient Mesopotamian Religion, Babylonian Magic and Sumerian Star-Gates...

Here is a Master Key to understanding the ancient mystical arts and the origins of religious spiritual traditions; true knowledge concerning the ordering and control of creation and manifestation in this Universe -- and the Anunnaki entities these arts are dedicated to. Their spirit remains strongly with us today.

Here is a New Standard Zuist Edition of the classic prayerbook compiled by Joshua Free; a revised and expanded pocket paperback version of the original "Book of Marduk by Nabu" (Liber-W) first published in 2010 as a practical companion to the titles available in this Zuism series as: "Anunnaki Gods: The Sumerian Religion" (Liber-50) and, of course, "Anunnaki Bible: The Cuneiform Scriptures."

TABLET OF CONTENTS

INTRODUCTION TO THE ZUIST EDITION

by Joshua Free

The Mardukite Chamberlains (Mardukite Research Organization) completed its Year-1 cycle of work in early 2010—and those efforts culminated into an anthology first released as "*Necronomicon: The Anunnaki Bible*"—but which, for a recent solidification of our tradition as Mardukite Zuism, has also been published as "*The Complete Anunnaki Bible*"; and even a newly revised pocket-portable abridged format, "*Anunnaki Bible: The Cuneiform Scriptures (New Standard Zuist Edition)*," is available. That culmination of material has certainly earned its recognition as a critical staple and source book for a modern Mardukite revival, even now, over a decade later.

Although a necessary foundation to work from, completion of the Year-1 (2009) work proved to be only a beginning for the route that would carry and build a global underground spiritual movement, now, into the 2020's and beyond with a revitalized "religious brand" as *Mardukite Zuism* and its very effective *Systemology* of applied spiritual technology. Much of this would not have been possible—or even coherently relevant—were it not for the pivotal Year-2 (2010) continuation of efforts made by "Chamberlains Alumni," those that dedicated another year of attention to the practical esoteric interpretation of the "*Anunnaki Bible*" and its background.

In 2010, the "Mardukite Chamberlains" began publishing an esoteric history series by Joshua Free, establishing stronger foundations for the modern revival interest. This included "Liber-50" (released as "*Sumerian Religion*" and "*The Gates of the Necronomicon*"), "Liber-W" ("*The Book of Marduk by Nabu*") and "Liber-M" ("*Maqlu Ritual Book*")—all of which have been reissued as 10th Anniversary Collector's Hardcovers. "Liber-50" is also available as "*Anunnaki Gods: The Sumerian Religion*" (New Standard Zuist Edition). "Liber-M" is also available as "*Anunnaki Rites: The Maqlu Ritual Book*" (New Standard Zuist Edition).

The "*Book of Marduk by Nabu*" reflects a very real modern *philosophy* and *metaspirituality* that is aligned specifically with the *Anunnaki* paradigm. However, materials from "*The Book of Marduk*" (*Liber-W*) in addition to other prayers, invocations and hymns from "*The Complete Anunnaki Bible*" have not yet appeared in any "New Standard Zuist Editions" prepared in the past couple of years. To correct this, we now present the premiere edition of "*Anunnaki Prayers: The Cuneiform Almanac.*"

FOREWORD TO THE NEW ZUIST EDITION

"The Gates-Games of Marduk"
by David Zibert

The esoteric concept of *"Gates"*—*Gateways* or *Star-Gates*—is a central theme in Babylonian lore and its later derivatives. Oftentimes, these are symbolically interpreted by "mystics" and "magicians" as *Thresholds* connecting between alternate (or parallel) "dimensions," "planes" or "realities."

During most occult initiation processes, the *Seeker* is guided through a series of specific dramatic ceremonial enactments in the Physical Universe that are intended to correlate with a Spiritual Universe, as per the famous Hermetic doctrine of "AS ABOVE, SO BELOW,"[1] leading an initiate through a kind of labyrinthine spiritual/mind maze —a "game" whereby the magician or priest seeks Ascension by moving through such symbolic *Gateways* and *Tunnels*.[2] These types of "games" are often referred to as "Magickal Pathworking"

---

1   While famously attributed to Hermes Trismegistus, this quote is originally found on an older Babylonian *cuneiform* tablet; see *"Tablets of Destiny (Revelation)"* (*Liber-One*) by Joshua Free.

2   Different semantics exist for the concept of *Gates* (described here) in every ancient culture across the globe. These may be readily and easily researched, if the *Seeker* is so inclined.

or *Gatewalking*. Such a concept, in one form or another, will undoubtedly be already familiar to those acquainted with the occult underground; yet many times, a modern practitioner is likely to overlook the actual nature and significance of these *Gates*.

Sure enough, the very use of "*Gate*" semantics— *Thresholds*, *Portals* or any kind of *Door*—to represent another dimension or reality, is merely a *symbol* for the mind (or control center) to process data from a higher frequency of *Beingness*—the data coming from the *other side* of the *Gate*— down to the physical (*beta*) reality. A *symbol* is never the "thing" symbolized. The *symbol* is a *symbol*; and that is all there is to it.

> *Symbols* are frequently misunderstood
> *to be* equal to that which they represent.

So, this begs-the-question: Why exactly are practitioners using semantics and symbols of *Gates* in the first place? What is a *Gate*? A kind of *doorway*? Okay, what then about that?Perhaps a "door" is a type of intermediary *opening* between two different places or points in space...maybe? That seems rather legit if looking at and considering a bit of the aforementioned "games" and how they work—and these can get pretty involved; and there's nothing wrong with that. *Except for one point*: that's not actually what a "door" is at all!

And those beings—those who designed the rules of this "game" are taking great care that everyone is too distracted by the systems to notice that. They are, in fact, counting on this to keep the "game" alive. Simply stated:

A "*door*" is a willfully built and directed *opening* through a willfully built and directed *barrier.*

That's all there is to *that*. Now, apply *that* to the "games" being played out in this universe, and realize how someone, somewhere, has intentionally put those barriers up, making you believe that he's some kind of authority over yourself, the real Self, and that you absolutely have to move through some maze like a mouse to see the Light at the end of the tunnel, when all you have to do is simply take back responsibility for playing the "game" and remove these barriers you were enforced to be in agreement with; to actually meet-up with your true Self and realize that in the holistic nature of spiritual (*Alpha*)[3] existence, that the "Clear Light" was there all along. *Do you see that?*

---

3   Semantics of "Alpha" and "Beta" existence and "control centers" are derived from "*Mardukite Systemology*" materials; "*Mardukite Zuism: A Brief Introduction*" is found in this present book.

* * * * * * *

The way the "game" of physical (*beta*) reality is set up is demonstrated in the Babylonian *Epic of Creation*—the *Enuma Eliš*—where MARDUK endeavored to order the physical (*beta*) universe/ reality through what is described as the fashioning and sealing of *Gates*. The famous *Epic* relates how control over the game of reality is somehow bound to the control of some nebulous "*Tablets of Destiny*," which, in the beginning, are in possession of TIAMAT.

The *Enuma Eliš* is not only the Archetypal *Epic of Creation*, it's also the Archetypal "*Fantasy Adventure*" where a hero goes to slay an evil dragon in order to retrieve a magical treasure. TIAMAT is the "evil one" in this instance, but more accurately, she has the *Tablets of Destiny*—and MARDUK succeeded in convincing his fellow *Anunnaki* to agree for him to direct his attention toward being the maker of the rules, the setter of barriers—the "*Game-Master.*" In view of the *Epic*: should MARDUK succeed in slaying the dragon, he is promised to have ultimate authority over creation, bypassing the Cosmic Law of causality by somehow getting the other *Anunnaki*—and then later on, *Humanity*—to willfully agree to said authority; the very way to make up the rules...

"The ANUNNAKI told MARDUK:
Thy fate is unequaled, thy word is ANU.
Your words shall be command,
In your power shall it be to exalt and to
  abase.
None among the gods shall transgress your
  boundary."

—*"Enuma Eliš,"* Tablet-IV

"The ANUNNAKI set out a garment
And continued to speak to MARDUK.
'May thy fate, O lord, be supreme among
  the gods,
To destroy and to create; speak only the
  word,
And your command shall be fulfilled.
Command now that the garment vanish;
Speak the word again and let the garment
  reappear!'
Then he spake the words and the garment
  vanished;
Again he commanded it and the garment
  reappeared."

—*"Enuma Eliš,"* Tablet-IV

Even before engaging KINGU and TIAMAT in
battle, it is seen that the powers of MARDUK
come first from his own *Self-Determinism* to act—
and be at *Cause*—in the political-play of the

"*gods.*" MARDUK is described as the *only* member of the *Anunnaki* willing to take any *Responsibility* in this matter. By doing so, he directs his *Will* "against all odds" in a grand attempt to become the rule-maker of the "game":

> "All the *gods* have turned to [TIAMAT], with those, whom you created,
> They go to her side. I sent ANU,
>   but he could not withstand her;
> NUDIMMUD⁴ was afraid and turned back.
> But MARDUK has set out, the champion of the gods, your son;
> To set out against TIAMAT his heart has called him."
>
> —*Enuma Eliš,*" Tablet-III

> "If I [MARDUK], your avenger,
> Conquer TIAMAT and give you life, […]
> With my word in place, I will decree fate.
> May whatsoever I do remain unaltered,
> May the word of my lips never be changed nor made to no avail."
>
> —*Enuma Eliš,*" Tablet-III

---

4 An alternate name for ENKI, meaning "*The Fashioner.*"

Now I hope this won't be a spoiler for newcomers, but MARDUK does successfully gain control of the *Tablets of Destiny,* simultaneously killing TIAMAT and her brood. MARDUK's overtaking of physical reality is clear as TIAMAT loses touch with the consensual reality that she just previously had dominion over, the tablets stating: "[…] she acted possessed and lost her sense of reason." The remainder of the *Epic* describes how MARDUK set up rules of his own by "*postulating*" a reality based on agreements about "*barriers,*" or else, *something to be free from*—pretty carceral[5] stuff alright: the *Gates* system—or *Matrix*—underlying physical (*beta*) reality to this day. But, MARDUK is a clever fellow—and, of course, he just left the *Key* to the *Locks* around for us, in plain sight:

> "With the *Key* known only to my *Race.*
>   Let none enter that *Gate,*
> Since to invoke *Death* is to utter the final
>   prayer."
>
> —"*Enuma Eliš,*" Tablet-VI

So while it might seem to some that the efforts of MARDUK relayed within the *Enuma Eliš* is what has entrapped humanity into this existence as some kind of "evil demiurge"—which is the view taken by the original "Gnostics" and their derivati-

---

5   "*Carceral*" – of, or pertaining to, a prison or imprisonment.

ves—it is not so. The Babylonian *Epic of Creation* is rather a gift of MARDUK to humanity. It contains the *Keys* of reality systematization and its engineering; how it is done, but also how it can be undone.

These *Arcane Tablets* composing the *Creation Epic* relate, quite simply, "*Creation*"—that is, something willfully and purposefully "made" by an *Awareness*. We are now able to clearly see the systematic pattern behind such Creation, then undo and redo it under full *Responsibility of Self*.

And that's what "Mardukite Systemology" *is*.

That is what is meant by "using ancient wisdom to unlock human potential."

MARDUK is thus the Archetypal *Alpha Spirit*[6] incarnated. Here is why it is said, in the celebrated Mardukite Incantation of Eridu: "It is not I, but MARDUK who commands the incantation." This method does not mean a surrendering of the Self to an outside force that is personified by a godform. it is taking back contact with the real *Self*—

---

6 *"Alpha Spirit"* – a spiritual lifeform; the True Self or "I-AM"; the spirit that is controlling the physical body (genetic vehicle) using a Lifeline, or continuum, of spiritual "ZU" energy. Refer to *"Mardukite Zuism: A Brief Introduction."*

the *Alpha Self*—of which MARDUK is a demonstration of.

Actuality of the literal events in the tale itself becomes irrelevant; because a workable method of reaching higher realities has been drawn from it.

And what is workable *is* true.

The *Enuma Eliš* is not only the *Epic of Creation* for a Physical (*Beta*) Universe, but also the *creation of human ability* to reclaim Self. Everyone carries within Self the potential to be MARDUK. This means you and I, here and now, have the right to awaken this potential as it was foretold on these *Arcane Tablets*.

It has always been there.

All you have to do is *remember*.

> S*pirit of the Earth, remember!*
> *Spirit of the Sky, remember!*

~ David Zibert
Master Mardukite of Canada
Council of Nabu-Tutu
Systemology A.T. Lab Office, Québec
Summer Solstice 2021

MARDUKITE

ZUISM

A BRIEF
INTRODUCTION

*According to the most ancient
historical records
written at the birth of our
modern civilization...* *

432,000 YEARS AGO...*

a small population of advanced beings—called the <u>ANUNNAKI</u>—began developing the planet Earth for their purposes. These elite Self-Actualized spiritual beings resided on Earth in physical bodies, but found their forms inadequate for the physical labors required. Enter: the "Human Condition." Ancient "<u>cuneiform</u>" tablet writings from Sumerians and Babylonians of Mesopotamia are clear regarding the original creation and systematic programming of Humanity.

CUNEIFORM...

is the oldest known writing system used by scribes of ancient Babylon to record their wisdom and the history of humanity on <u>clay tablets</u>. "Cuneiform" is named for its style of wedge-shaped script formed by a <u>reed pen</u> called a "<u>stylus.</u>" Rather than an alphabet of letters, cuneiform is a system of "<u>signs</u>" representing "things" and "ideas." These may be combined to represent even more complex "signs."

---

*   Version 1.1 – First published in 2019 as "*Mardukite Zuism: A Brief Introduction*" in booklet form.

Many concepts adopted for modern "Mardukite Zuism" are derived from cuneiform tablets. The ANUNNAKI introduced complex writing systems in order to program civilization and all parameters of Reality for the Human Condition. Legendary "Tablets of Destiny" (Divine Truth, supreme knowledge and cosmic power of the "gods") were first introduced to Humanity in the Babylonian narrative known best as the "Epic of Creation.

THE ARCANE TABLETS.

Ancient Babylonians used the Tablets of Destiny & Creation Epic to systematize all cosmic knowledge into a workable paradigm called "Mardukite Zuism"—a systemology received directly from the ANUNNAKI.

Paradigm : an all-encompassing standard or religion used to view the world and communicate reality.

Systemology : applied philosophies of Mardukite Zuism combined with personal spiritual techniques and technology ("Tech") that is effectively demonstrating systematic principles of a "paradigm."

THE EPIC OF CREATION.

Seven cuneiform tablets compose the ancient
<u>Babylonian Epic of Creation</u>, named the <u>Enuma
Eliš</u> by scholars after its opening lines. These
seven tablets are the basis for what later traditions refer to as the *"Seven Days of Creation."*
The *Epic of Creation* tablets describe development of all existences with a Divine artistic
perfection. The Enuma Eliš is the core example
of religious literature from Babylon, which
served as the basis for ancient *"Mardukite
Zuism"*—the first true systematized religion in
history.

THE SYSTEMOLOGY OF LIFE,
UNIVERSES & EVERYTHING.

The *Arcane Tablets* describe the division of the
ALL by the LAW, outside of which is but IN-
FINITY. The *Epic of Creation* describes these
activities as "mythology."

The Mardukite Systemology "Standard Model"
uses the same information to demonstrates...

that <u>ALL</u> ("AN-KI") envelops both:
the <u>Spiritual Existences</u> ("AN")
and the <u>Physical Existences</u> ("KI")
divided by <u>Cosmic Law</u> and
connected by <u>Life-Awareness</u> ("ZU")
and beyond which is only the <u>Abyss</u>,
an <u>Infinity of Nothingness</u> ("ABZU").

ANCIENT SUMERIAN DEFINITIONS.

<u>ABZU</u> = "Abyss" ("Nothingness")
<u>ZU</u> = "Spiritual Life" ("Awareness")
<u>ANKI</u> = "All Existences" ("Existence")
<u>AN</u> = "Spiritual Universe" ("Heaven")
<u>KI</u> = "Physical Universe" ("Earth")

ALTERNATE MARDUKITE NEXGEN SYSTEMOLOGY DEFINITIONS.

<u>ABZU</u> = "Infinity of Nothingness"
<u>ZU</u> = "Awareness of Alpha Spirit"
<u>ANKI</u> = "The Standard Model"
<u>AN</u> = "Alpha Existence" ("Spiritual")
<u>KI</u> = "Beta Existence" ("Physical")

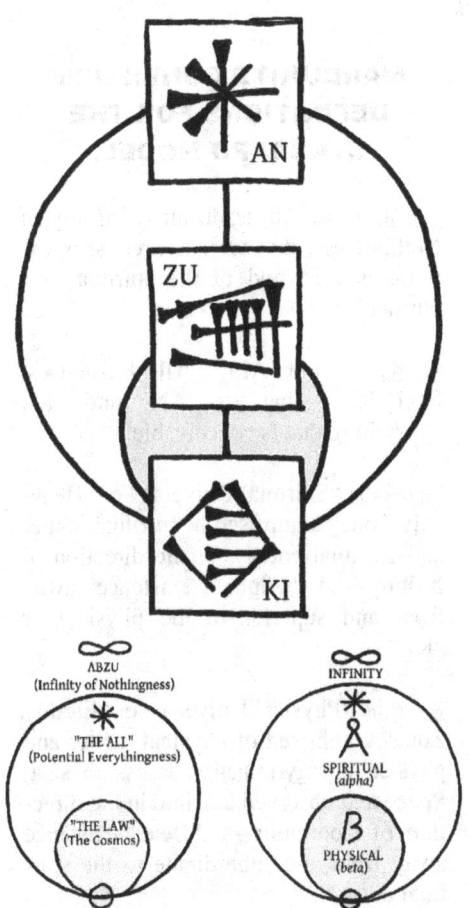

AN

ZU

KI

∞
ABZU
(Infinity of Nothingness)

✳
"THE ALL"
(Potential Everythingness)

"THE LAW"
(The Cosmos)

∞
INFINITY

✳

𝛂
SPIRITUAL
(alpha)

𝛃
PHYSICAL
(beta)

MARDUKITE CUNEIFORM DEFINITIONS FOR THE STANDARD MODEL.

<u>ABZU</u> = the Abyss; Infinity; Infinity of Nothingness; that which extends, is exterior and beyond of the spiritual and physical.

<u>ANKI</u> = the ALL; All Existences; Everything that is AN and KI; Everything that is conceivable.

<u>AN</u> = the "Spiritual Universe" or "Heavenly Zone" comprised of spiritual matter and spiritual energy, in the direction of Infinity—an "Alpha" existence away from and superior to the physical or "KI."

<u>KI</u> = the "Physical Universe" or "Earthly Zone" comprised of physical matter and physical energy in action across physical Space and observed as Time in the direction of Continuity—a "Beta" existence away from and subordinate to the spiritual or "AN."

<u>ZU</u> = "to know"; "knowingness"; "Awareness" or "consciousness"; spiritual energy and matter of AN that is observed as "Lifeforce" in KI; "Spiritual Life Energy"; the actual personal spiritual Identity or "Awareness" of Self as Spirit which extends along a "line" from the Spiritual Universe (AN) to the Physical Universe (KI).

THE TABLETS OF DESTINY & BABYLONIAN CREATION EPIC.

The Absolute behind ALL Existence is referred to on the *Tablets of Destiny* as the Infinity of Nothingness. It is the only constant static of latent unmanifest potentiality of ALL and Everythingness.

The LAW—Cosmic Law—is defined as the Cosmic Dragon—TIAMAT—on "Epic of Creation" Tablets. She is the First Cause or movement across a "Sea of Infinity." Later, the LAW becomes a division between Spiritual Existence ("AN") and any Physical Universe ("KI"). The LAW—Tiamat—permeating ALL, uses the *Tablets of Destiny* and then fixes the systems of finite potential: The Systems of Manifestation—Substance, Motion and Awareness.

"Before heaven or earth are named," the formation and interaction of active existences —"substances" and "bodies" and "Life" and "gods"—creates turbulence and waves of action through space. The governing system of Cosmic Law—Tiamat—responds accordingly. She fixes the Tablets of Destiny to her "deputy"—a messenger wave action of the LAW named "Kingu" and sends him rippling out to "meet" the Anunnaki "gods."

The Anunnaki Assembly of "gods" prepare to battle The LAW. When none among them comes forth to engage, it is the Anunnaki "god" MARDUK that volunteers as hero to confront Kingu and Tiamat—but with a condition that the Anunnaki Assembly recognize him as "Chief of the Gods" upon his success.

When MARDUK approaches the LAW directly, he is flanked by Kingu and the "army of Ancient Ones." MARDUK is able to relinquish the Tablets of Destiny from Kingu. With the Tablets of Destiny, Marduk conquers a true understanding of Cosmic Law and thereby Tiamat.

THE TABLETS OF DESTINY
& SELF-HONESTY.

Marduk uses the Tablets of Destiny to discover "Self-Honesty" and Divine Knowledge governing "Cosmic Ordering"—systems dividing the "Spiritual Universe" (AN) from a "Physical Universe" (KI). The two universes are connected only by a stream of Spiritual Lifeforce Awareness that Sumerians called ZU. Wisdom from the Arcane Tablets is later passed down to and concealed by an ancient esoteric secret society in Babylon: the Scribes, High Priests and Priestesses of Mardukite Zuism.

Self-Honesty is a term describing an original "Alpha" state of clear knowingness and Self-directed beingness."Self-Honesty" is the most basic and true expression of Self as "I-AM"— free of artificial attachments; reactive-response conditioning; and imposed or enforced programming as Reality for the Human Condition. Spiritual development in modern *Mardukite Zuism* is referred to as the "Pathway to Self-Honesty" and the "Gateway to Infinity." It is modeled directly from the Ancient Mystery Tradition observed at the Temples of Babylon.

THE KEY TO THE GATE.

"I will take my Blood—and with Bone—I will fashion a Race of Humans to keep Watch of the Gate. And from the Blood of Kingu I will create another Race of Humans to inhabit the Earth in service to the Gods—so shrines to the Anunnaki may be built and the temples filled. I will bind the Elder Gods to the Watchtowers; let them keep watch over the Gate of Abzu and the Gate of Tiamat and Gate of Kingu—and with a Key that shall be ever hidden, known to none, except only to my Mardukites." —MARDUK, *Enuma Elis, Creation Tablet VI.*

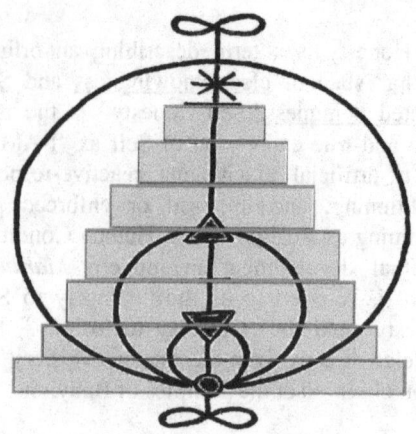

THE ANUNNAKI LADDER OF LIGHTS & BABYLONIAN GATEWAYS TO INFINITY.

ZIGGURAT TEMPLES in Babylonia—and throughout Mesopotamia—served to remind populations of the ZU connecting "Heaven" and "Earth."

Seven-stepped "levels" of the physical ZIG-GURAT TEMPLES of Babylonia—and seven corresponding Gates—represent spiritual levels of actualized Awareness; states of Self-purifica-tion (or "spiritual defragmentation") as they ascend in the direction of AN toward Infinity of Supreme Beingness—the Pathway of Self-Hon-esty—in imitation of the footsteps of the gods during their descent through the "spheres" or "Gates."

COSMOLOGY AND METAPHYSICS.

All Things in the Physical Universe are in mo-tion—wave motions of "energy and matter in space measured as-and-across time." Continuity of the Physical Universe (KI) is divided by LAW and encompassed by the ALL (ANKI).

The direction of AN extends toward ABZU, an Infinity of Nothingness beyond effective existence.

The true <u>Alpha Self</u> is a source—the "spiritual cause" of "physical effects." It engages a <u>Self-determined WILL</u> from its "spiritual" <u>Alpha existence</u> to actualize Awareness for "physical" <u>Beta existence</u> experience as "Life."

USING ANCIENT WISDOM TO UNLOCK HUMAN POTENTIAL.

Communication of clear wisdom and true knowledge from Arcane Tablets is distorted as it passes through time and geography, diverse languages and authoritarian cultures using the "Power" to program the masses and fragment the Human Condition away from Self-Honesty.

Use of this ancient wisdom reveals the Keys to "<u>Cosmic Ordering</u>"—applying the highest Self-directed understanding of "cause-and-effect" sequences in the Physical Universe.

MARDUKITE ZUISM, SYSTEMOLOGY & SPIRITUALITY.

The Spiritual Universe (AN)—of metaphysical or spiritual energy and metaphysical or spiritual matter is not dependent on the Physical Universe (KI) to exist; the two are existentially independent of each other, maintaining a single channel, conduit or connection, which is <u>Alpha Spirit</u> "Awareness" as Spiritual Life or ZU. The Alpha Spirit engages a <u>ZU-line</u>, a spiritual lifeline of ZU energy to a genetic vehicle or organic body to experience physical beta existence.

MARDUKITE ZUISM DEFINITIONS FOR SYSTEMOLOGY.

<u>ALPHA SPIRIT</u> = a spiritual lifeform; the True Self or "I-AM"; the spirit that is controlling the physical body or "genetic vehicle" using a Lifeline or continuum of spiritual "ZU" energy.

<u>ASCENSION</u> = actualized Awareness elevated to (AN) spiritual existence that is exterior to beta-existence.

<u>BETA-EXISTENCE</u> = manifestation in the Physical Universe (KI); the state of existence or condition of frequency specific to physical energy and physical matter in physical space.

<u>FRAGMENTATION</u> = breaking into parts; fractioning wholeness; fracture of holism; discontinuity; separation; outside the state of Self-Honesty.

<u>GENETIC VEHICLE</u> = a physical life-form; the physical (beta) body controlled by the (Alpha) Spirit using a continuous Lifeline of ZU energy.

<u>HUMAN CONDITION</u> = a default programmed conditioned state standard issue Human existence/experience.

<u>ZU-LINE</u> = a spectrum of Spiritual Life-Energy (ZU); an energetic channel or Identity-Continuum connecting Alpha Spirit Awareness from Infinity-to-Infinity including the full physical beta range.

THE HIGHEST FORM OF
TRUE DIVINE WORSHIP.

The true Destiny of Humanity is to achieve spiritual <u>Self-Actualization</u>; the reunion of Self with the Divine. Attaining Self-Honesty in this Life is the most important step a person can take toward achieving their highest ideals, goals and realizations.

The Highest form of "True Worship" begins with the Spirit—the true Self—and all external practices, rituals, ceremonies and historical examples are but outer reflections of this ideal. The Highest form of "Sin" is against the Spirit —against the Self—and its ability to maintain Self-Honesty. There are modes of thought, action and Self-direction of effort that will contribute toward Ascension; and modes that lead away from that.

Beta experiences of "Sin"—pain, fear, guilt, anger—are all related to personal fragmentation; and emotional turbulence from all of these may be released—and intention energy redirected— because: <u>we are all co-creators of Reality in this lifetime!</u>

SPHERES OF EXISTENCE, INFLUENCE & UTILITARIAN ETHICS OF SYSTEMOLOGY.

The prime directive of all beta existence is: *to exist*. The continuation of existence is the purpose behind all existence. Between realization of Self and Infinity, there are many spheres of existence that we may influence. All of the spheres are interconnected.

There is nothing in existence that is in absolute exclusion to all existence. Each sphere of existence supports subsequent existences and assists reaches toward higher spheres of influence.

The greatest good contributes to the greatest continuation of optimum existence for the greatest sphere of inclusion. Degrees of rightness and wrongness are determined by Cosmic Law and are reflected in the quality of, and continuation of, an optimal existence at the highest sphere of existence.

Individual happiness is attained via the channel to the highest sphere. Human unhappiness is the result of "selfishness" and/or lack of "spiritual Self-Actualization" and "Awareness."

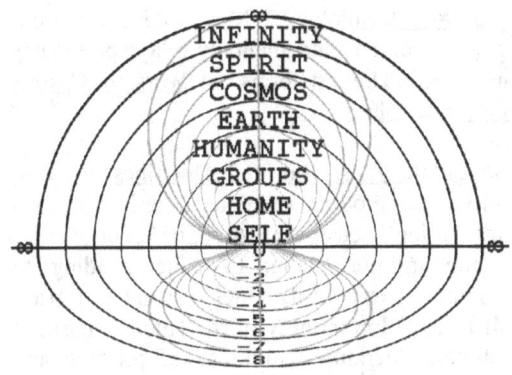

ZU : MARDUKITE ZUISM & MODERN ZUIST RELIGION.

History demonstrates how dangerous, trouble-some and easily misused the concept of "REL-GION" is; so, for purposes of incorporating Mardukite Zuism as a contemporary standard, the idea of "religion" is here treated as:

> a concise spiritual paradigm, set of be-liefs and practices, regarding Divinity, Infinite Beingness—or else "God."

Mardukite Zuism operates under a premise of very specific beliefs and a "systemology" of "spiritual technology." Mardukite Zuist Religious Doctrine fundamentally relays previously described "Highest forms" of Worship, Cosmic Law, and Ethics.

Mardukite Zuist Spiritual Doctrines successfully meet modern religious criteria for: a) a description of cosmic creation; b) belief in a Supreme Infinite Being; c) ethics leading to Human Ascension; d) ethics of conduct toward all Life; e) Immortality of the Human Spirit; f) religious literature, traditions of practice and spiritual advisement.

GOALS & IDEALS OF MARDUKITE ZUISM.

The word "ZU" meant "knowing" in original Sumerian cuneiform script. Goals and ideals of Zuism reflect this. Mardukite Zuism seeks to assist an individual in reclaiming a realization of the True Self or "I-AM" as the Immortal Spirit, in line with a most ancient directive: to "Know Thyself."

In view of the fact that all modern humans are subjected to technologies depriving them of their freedoms to *be, think, know* and pursue truth: the goals and ideals of Zuism are to effectively revive and repair these very abilities and certainties of the Individual—as an increase of "Actualized Awareness."

INFINITY, "GOD" & SUPREME BEINGNESS

The Spiritual Philosophy of Zuism is systematized by a Standard Model. It demonstrates Absolute Supreme Beingness associated with the Highest realization of "God" as INFINITY. No thing is Higher or Absolute than the Infinity of Nothing—and reducing Supreme Beingness to any finite personality or character trait is to limit and defile with lesser "words."

The Highest Name of God cannot be conceived —hence our symbolic use of the Infinity Sign:

∞

...or Sumerian cuneiform word-sign: "ABZU" —"The Infinite Nothingness and Source of All ZU."

The Spiritual Universe (AN) is *All-as-One* because it exists as an infinite singularity or stasis:

infinite potential with no gradient or observed motion; which is its own continuity.

The Physical Universe (KI) is *All-as-One* because it is in continuous motion, with all manifest parts working systematically as a continuity of beta-existence.

A "spiritual continuum" or "conduit channel" of ZU—absolute energy from the Spiritual Universe (AN)—links our Awareness levels of "I-AM," "True Self" or Spirit ("Alpha Spirit") with the degrees of motion and variation in the Physical Universe.

This Alpha Spirit or "Soul" is the true Awareness, "I" or "Self" connected to the operation and control of the physical body.

THE TRUE HUMAN ALPHA SPIRIT.

The true Self is the "I" or "Spirit" regardless of its position, degree or level of Awareness. Spirit remains. Whatever "spiritual energy-matter" composes the Alpha Spirit or "soul"—it must occupy this "other space" with its spiritual existence and then project its Awareness and Will onto the Physical Universe (KI) in order to experience the Game we call Life.

This "spiritual energy-matter" that composes all Life (as a Lifeforce with Awareness and Consciousness) goes by many names throughout history—but we find the idea first treated as <u>ZU</u> on cuneiform tablets of Mesopotamia.

On an Identity lifeline of ZU energy, all Alpha Spirits are operating from a Spiritual Universe. We refer to this as the ZU-line on the Standard Model.

ZU is the name given to the spiritual essence of all Life in existence—and Self is a concentrated center or focal point as a ZU-continuum or Identity.

The True Self of an Individual Human is a "spiritual universe cause" of "physical universe effects"—engaging as an immortal Alpha Spirit with a Self-determined Will actualized as an Awareness along the ZU-continuum, extending from Infinity-to-Infinity, through every possible frequency and vibration along the total spectrum of physical and metaphysical existence.

THE SYSTEMOLOGY PRACTICES
OF SPIRITUAL ADVISEMENT
& COUNSELING SERVICES
FOR MARDUKITE ZUISM.

The Mardukite Chamberlains were established in 2009 dedicated to recovery and consolidation of all historical, scriptural & ritual records of ancient Babylon in Mesopotamia. In 2011, a Mardukite faction (International Systemology Society) began to research and develop methods to apply ancient wisdom as a futurist spiritual technology that awakens, unlocks and fully actualizes spiritual potential of the Human Condition.

A systematic approach to spirituality is seen on the Standard Model, where ZU-line frequencies are represented at various degrees: "zero-point" body death; cellular activity and sensory perceptions of a genetic body; bio-chemicals induced by emotion; thoughts and intention transmitted between our Alpha Spirit and the "genetic vehicle"—all the way "up" the scale to a perfected clarity of Self-Actualized Awareness of I-AM as our true "Alpha" state, just below Infinity and Absolute Beingness.Full potential of ZU in Consciousness is only altered from its natural state as a result of personal fragmentation of the Human Condition. This may be restored with spiritual practices.

The Pathway to Self-Honesty is a personal journey and spiritual adventure marked by progressive clearing of spiritual energy channels fragmented by the imprinting and programming accumulated from experiences in our environment—the "debris" that fragments the total actualized experience of Self in Awareness as the Alpha Spirit.

The first and most important step—Before an individual can actualize potentials of the Spirit as Self, they must fully realize: the I-AM Self and the Alpha Spirit are One.

This state of Knowingness is the primary intention of basic spiritual practices found in Mardukite Zuism.

"Systemology" books and advanced training courses are also available to Mardukite Ministers seeking to qualify as specialized clergy, priests, priestess, and systematic processing pilots.

CREED OF MARDUKITE ZUISM.
PRINCIPLES OF BELIEF. [*]

1.) We believe in an Absolute Beingness, which is Infinite—the ABZU—the All-as-One encompassing Source of All Being, Knowing and Awareness to all Alpha (Spiritual-AN) and Beta (Physical-KI) states of existence.

2.) We believe in a spiritual energy of all Life and Awareness—ZU—in the physical universe (beta) that is an effect of a spiritual (Alpha) cause; a Spirit that is cause. This Spirit—in its Alpha state—is the True Self "I-AM" Individual Identity that many have called the "soul."

3.) We believe that the Human Condition is a genetic vehicle used by a spiritual source (AN) to experience the Finite as physical existence (KI)—that we are Awareness (ZU) projected onto a genetic vehicle—and that while the vehicle/body may perish to physical entropy, the "Alpha Spirit" remains immortal and Self-directed to the extent of its own Actualized Awareness.

---

[*] First drafted in 2019.

4.) We believe that the highest form of worship and spirituality is the actualization and advancement of our "Self" as Spirit in Self-Honesty—and that Self-Honesty is the I-AM Alpha state of Being and Knowing, which is realizable in this lifetime.

5.) We believe that the purpose of all existence is: to exist—and that the prime directive of all spiritual Life is: continued existence of spiritual Life and co-creation of habitable Reality. "Good" and "Moral" actions are evaluated to the extent of this end.

6A.) We believe that no Life exists in exclusion to all other Life—and that the conditions of a habitable Reality extending from Self include:
Home; Community; All Humanity; All Life on Earth; All Life in the Universe; All Spiritual Life; and the Infinite.

6B.) We believe in a continued evolution of Alpha Spirit awareness developed beyond one physical life, and that a Spirit experiences many.

7A.) We believe Mardukite Zuism and its applied systemology is a 21st Century AD synthesis of the 21st Century BC wisdom collected on cuneiform tablets and experienced in ancient Mesopotamia, esp. Babylon.

7B.) This cuneiform library included details concerning: beings called the Anunnaki; ordering of the Cosmos; creation of Humanity; and an entire legacy of systematized traditions.

8.) We believe in the continuation of, and proper communication of, the true legacy of Human history—and the ability of every Human to realize that they are a Free Spirit in a Free Zone of Self-Determinism: and no "evils" can affect intentions if an individual is spiritually Self-Actualized in Self-Honesty.

THE ARCANE KNOWLEDGE FROM MARDUK'S TABLET OF DESTINY.*

1.) As above, so below;
On earth as it is in Heaven
an-bala ki-bala an-ba ki an-ba

2.) What the Mind believes, the Spirit reinforces
da-ga nam-ku-zu dingir-Lamma a bi-ib-gar

3.) When disaster is self-made,
no man can interfere
*nig-ku-lam-ma dingir-ra-na-ka su—
tu-tu nu-ub-zu*

4.) What is given in submission
is a catalyst for defiance
nig-gu-gar-ra nig-gaba-gar-ra

5.) Whoever partners with Truth, creates Life
nig-ge-na-ta a-ba in-da-di nam-ti i-u-tu

---

*   From *"Tablets of Destiny (Revelation)"* by Joshua Free.

THE EXPANDED BOOK OF

MARDUK

BY NABU

INTRODUCTION & APPLICATION
NABU-TUTU SERIES – TABLET IV

We have sealed seven representative stations or gates in BABYLON. While it is true that each of the cities emphasized their own local patrons—a god and a goddess—We have sought a unity for all the gods, under the watchful eye of my father, MARDUK, son of ENKI.

Our Father, ENKI, took MARDUK as an apprentice to the magical and religious arts while in E.RIDU and I later took hold of such mysteries and dispersed the knowledge to my scribes and priests in BABYLON and Egypt, where my family was recognized by other names.

The "Seven" are each embodiments of one of the seven gates forged in BABYLON, homes to the gods of the "younger pantheon." It is true, the same seven-fold division may be found to fragment the *world of form*—corresponding to color, sound, or the planets observed by the ancient ancestors from Earth, seen as *"Guardians."*

The seven planetary systems—which have been connected to the "Seven" of the Gates—also correlate to an easily observable cycle of Time. The planet-ruling days will offer the supplicant [priest] an intention ceremonial or meditative opportunity to appeal to each of the "sets" of ANUNNAKI "divine couples" honored in the "younger pantheon" of Babylon.

Sunday–*Sun*–SHAMMASH [UTU] (& AYA)
Monday–*Moon*–NANNA [SIN] (& NINGAL)
Tuesday–*Mars*–NERGAL (& ERESHKIGAL)
Wednesday–*Mercury*–NABU (& TESHMET)
Thursday–*Jupiter*–MARDUK (& SARPANIT)
Friday–*Venus*–ISHTAR-INANNA (& DUMUZI)
Saturday–*Saturn*–NINIB [NINURTA] (& BA'U)

Within the combined domains of the "Seven" are all of the material and spiritual aspects a priest or magician seeks in life (such as: ISHTAR for *love* or SHAMMASH for *truth*) and one merely must appeal with Self-Honesty and true words to attain them. This is as the original arts were set down in days of old, left for men to remember us—and we will remember you.

The Names and Gates are not merely there for bedazzlement of "occult initiates" as you have been taught by others—there to ascend in half-measures and then forget about—they are very real "magical skills" and "spiritual lessons" based on the division and the fragmentation of the material universe—a mastery only attainable by a true and faithful relationship with the ANUNNAKI gods of your ancestors.

Man's use of the spiritual power of the gods became subverted, altered and bastardized into the mystical systems now given for your disposal, written by men with no better understanding of the traditions they seek to invoke then those who read them. (And some of these traditions have even falsely said to be derived from my hand by whatever name is attributed to me.) The true priest or magician compels the gods by friendship and trust, not fear and hatred.

From MARDUK, I learned the power of incantation. These secrets I learned in ERIDU. I was taught to appease the gods in his name, to speak the words of the higher. MARDUK invoked the name of ENKI, our father, who, invoked the name of ANU. And so was born the magical "hierarchies" that magicians have confused. I taught the magician-scribes of my order to invoke my name and seal during their petitions to the gods, which I have given here, as I learned it from MARDUK. . .

THE GRAND INVOCATION
INCANTATION OF ERIDU

ANU above me, King in Heaven.
ENLIL, Commander of the Airs.
ENKI, Lord of the Deep Earth.
I am NABU – hear my words.
I am the priest of MARDUK and SARPANIT.
Son of Our father, ENKI and DAMKINA.
I am the priest in E.RIDU.
I am the magician in BABYLON.
My spell is the spell of ENKI.
My incantation is the incantation of MARDUK.
The Tablets of Destiny, I hold in my hands.
The Ankh (rod and ring) of ANU and ANTU,
  I hold in my hands.
The wisdom of ENLIL and NINLIL, I call to me.
The Magic Circle of ENKI and DAMKINA,
  I conjure about me.
SHAMMASH and AYA are before me.
NANNA-SIN and NINGAL are behind me.
NERGAL and ERESHKIGAL are at my right
  side.
NINIB-NINURTA and BA'U are at my left side.
Blessed light of ISHTAR and DUMUZI shines
  favorably upon my sacred work.
It is not I, but MARDUK, who performs the
  incantations.

As should become increasingly apparent to the contemporary population of the present age, the ANUNNAKI are powerful and influential, though often directly unseen, forces behind the reality of the life you exist in—as your ancestors were well aware of. If you work with us in conjunction with the natural flow of the universal energies, then you will come face to face with your true destiny—and invited home, again.

Discern your true-knowledge, learn the challenge of self-mastery, and then dear *Seeker*, resolve to walk with the gods among the stars, circumnavigating the illusions of this world which have been raised before you as a test of your existence.

When you have proven yourself before us,
we shall celebrate your arrival . . .

[*Here ends Nabu-Tutu Tablet IV*]

MONDAY — THE MOON
NANNA-SIN

To the ancients, the moon was the "sun at night."
It illuminated the path for travelers and kept watch
as the people slept. Just as the sun was invoked to
grant judgments of the daytime, the moon is given
the domain over the dreams of men.

Being the first spiritual threshold (Gate) between
earth and heaven, the moon is significantly linked
to the astral plane. The priestesses (and later
witches) of INANNA-ISHTAR revered the moon,
called NANNA by Sumerians or Sin to the Babylonians, as their sky-father and/or spiritual-mate.
ISHTAR literally was the "daughter of the moon"
(and a twin to the sun/SAMAS) and her followers
often also took this title.

Our pantheon places NANNA in the position of
lunar god with the designation of 30, the basic lunar month of the Sumerian calendar (30 x 12 =
360). The name NANNA (or NANNAR) is actually an attribute of the full moon. He is called Sin
(or SU.EN) when representing the crescent and the
name for the new moon is: *AS.IM.BABBAR*.

The lunar current is heavily water oriented with
blue hues, though best represented ritually in the
non-color spectrum (silver, black, white).

PRAYER TO NANNA & NINGAL
(BABYLONIAN)

ilu-NANNA. ilu-SIN. ilu-istari-NINGAL.
ilu-NANNAR. ilu-NAMRASIT.
su-bu-u man-za-za ina ilani rabuti maru aplu
  ilu-ENLIL u ilu-NINLIL
nam-rat urru-ka ina sami-i ina sat musi
du natalu, nasaru anabu harranu-dim
u nisu ina bitu sat musi suttu
itti namrasit ina sami-i
kima diparu, kima ilu-SAMAS
samsatu ilu-NANNA namaru suttu agu
abu ilu-SAMAS
rimi-nin-ni-ma anaku _____ , apil _____ ,
  sa ilu-sa ____ u ilu-istari-su _____ .
ilu-NANNA u ilu-NINGAL rimi-nin-ni-ma
kaparu anaku sillatu lu-us-tam-mar ilu-ut-ka
petu babu temu
li-iz-ziz ina imni-ya u sumuli-ya anaku
  arad-ka elu
an-un-na-ki ti-i-ru u na-an-za-zu

PRAYER TO NANNA & NINGAL
(ENGLISH)

NANNA. SIN. NINGAL.
NANNAR. MOON.
Mighty One among the gods, son of ENLIL
  and NINLIL,
Brightest in the heavens at night,
Keeping watch, protecting weary travelers
And the people in their homes as they sleep.
Your brightness extends through the heavens,
Like a torch – Like a fire-god.
Radiance of NANNA, who reflects the dreams
  of men,
To you was born the SUN.
Be favorable to me, I, __ son of __ , whose
  god is __ and whose goddess is __ .
May NANNA and NINGAL deal graciously
  with me,
Cleanse me of iniquity that I may be free to
  call upon thee.
Open the Gates of your mysteries to me,
Stand on either side of me, a servant of
  the Highest.
May the ANUNNAKI come forth and be
  established.

AN INVOCATION TO NANNA

Spirit of the Moon, SUEN [SIN], NANNA,
  The Mighty One,
SUEN, who is unique and bright among the
  ANUNNAKI gods,
The light gracing nations, exalted in Heaven
  and on Earth,
Be favorable to me, a Servant of the
  Covenant.
Bright is your light and brilliant is your torch,
  like the Fire-God
Your brightness extends to the ends of the
  Earth Planet.
ASIMBABBAR in the sky, of whose purpose
  no man can learn,
The fate of the universe is set before thee,
Gate of the Great Gate of the Spheres, open to
  me now.
God of the New Moon, whose purpose no
  man learns,
I have poured the offering of libation in the
  night and call to you.
I stand at the threshold of the Gateway of the
  Gods bowed down.
May my god and goddess, who have long
  been angry with me,

In the name of truth and justice,
I ask you to deal mercifully toward me.
Lady of Heaven & Earth,
In your splendor protect the Quadrangles.
I, __, son of __, whose god is __, and whose
   goddess is __,
May NABU answer my calls by the decree of
   your words.

TUESDAY — MARS — NERGAL

The martian current has always been one of the most difficult to properly relay on a spiritual basis. To emphasize the primal fiery destruction would be all too simple. The current is best correlated to the Sumerian concept of *"Girra"* or *"fires of God."* The "hand" of God requires a representative vehicle in which to exercise even its own power in physical ways. It represents the destructiveness of our past.

Underlying the power of Mars, and the demonstrator of this force in Babylon (NERGAL), is really "passion." The outer demonstrations of this pure attribute are what can later be deemed by men as lust, love, anger, jealousy and the like. But these are outer forms only – it is the passion, pure and true, that must be embraced.

NERGAL is invoked, then, to temper the visions of anger or discord in our lives so we might embrace the passion beneath with clarity, which is anything but evil or destructive. The number of NERGAL is 8, showing that he is outside of the "heavenly" ranks (ending in 5 or 0). His abode is with ERESHKIGAL, who is Queen in the "Underworld." Combined, the pair represent the most "gothic," misunderstood and yet truly romantic elements and attributes of divinity and creation: passion and death.

PRAYER TO NERGAL & ERESHKIGAL
(BABYLONIAN)

ilu-NERGAL. ilu-IRRIGAL.
   ilu-istari-ERESHKIGAL. ilu-ERRA.
siru belu ersetu
ilu-istari-ERESHKIGAL, beltu ersetu
saqu-su manzazu it-ti ilani samu
ilu-NERGAL u ilu-istari-ERESHKIGAL
rimi-nin-ni-ma, ana-ku ___ , apil ____ ,
   sa ilu-su ___ ilu-istar-su ____ .
banu-ya libbu alalu
di-ni uzzu ina ramanu libbu
ana-ku izuzzu mahru ze
petu babu temu
rimi-nin-ni-ma ina damu u du lemnutu seg
   ina ramanu zi
ana-ku arad-ka elu kamazu ze rimi-nin-ni-ma
babu-mah du pataru
an-un-na-ki ti-i-ru u na-an-za-zu

PRAYER TO NERGAL & ERESHKIGAL (ENGLISH)

NERGAL. IRRIGAL. ERESHKIGAL.
ERRA. MARS.
Exalted Lord of the Underworld.
ERESHKIGAL, Queen of the Underworld.
Great is your place among the gods of
   heaven.
NERGAL and ERESHKIGAL,
Truly have mercy on me, ___ , son of ___ ,
   whose god is ___ , whose goddess is ___ .
May your hearts be tempered.
Temper also the anger within my heart,
That I may stand before you,
Make me perfect to call upon you,
Open the Gates of your understanding to me.
Grant me a favorable death and keep evil
   from me in life.
I, a servant of the Highest, kneel before thee,
   take pity on me.
May the Great Doors stand open.
May the ANUNNAKI return and be
   established.

AN INVOCATION TO NERGAL

Mighty Lord NERGAL, hero of the peoples,
First-born of NU.NAM.NIR,
Prince of ENLIL among the ANUNNAKI and
*   Lord of War.*
I call to thee from the Gate and Sphere of the
*   Sun,*
Hear me, Lord of the Underworld, consort to
*   ERESHKIGAL.*
NERGAL, Strong Arm of the ANUNNAKI
*   and IGIGI,*
When you traverse the bright heavens, your
*   place is lofty.*
Spirit of the Gate of the Dead, hear me:
Swing wide the Gate for me, __, son of __,
*   whose god is __, and whose goddess is __,*
Since you have been beneficent to me, I honor
*   your divinity,*
In your compassion and mercy, may your
*   angry heart have rest.*
Turn back with your Horrible Weapons and
*   maintain peace.*
Spirit of the Gate of the ARRA and AGGA,
*   open to me.*
Let your name be heralded with humility
*   among the people.*

WEDNESDAY — MERCURY — NABU

The *Mercurial* current is connected to divination: relaying information through the universe, or else, communication. Whether it is prayers, a song, the recording of history or the prediction of the future, the performance is undertaken by the blessing of the "scribe-messenger" of the gods. "*Thoth*" or "*Hermes*" is sometimes identified for this current, demonstrating the connection to magic systems, occultism and the air element. Babylonian tradition observes me, NABU, as son of MARDUK, as the scribe-priest of the gods, the keeper of the "destinies" among the younger pantheon with the designation of 12 (connecting heavenly-time and earth-time).

My scribe-priests worked diligently during the Babylonian era forging tablet texts based on the Sumerian tradition, supporting our local patron, MARDUK, as *King of the Gods*, usurping the position of ENLIL and usurping the rights of the position by NINURTA for both spiritual reasons and physical politics. This is presently being resolved energetically, demonstrating the power of knowledge, true or false, and how it can be used to shape the Human Condition and thereby the world. Invoke my name for clarity and discernment in the seeking of truth. My color is blue.

PRAYER TO NABU & TESHMET
(BABYLONIAN)

ilu-NABU. ilu-TUTU. ilu-istari-TESHMET
ilu-istari-TASMIT. ilu-NEBOS.
tupsarru si-mat ilani
sarru nam-zu si-mat ilani
asaridu bukur ilu-MARDUK u ilu-SARPANIT
ilu-NABU na-as duppu si-mat ilani
ramanu ur-hi suttu lid-mi-ik
ilu-NABU u ilu-TASMITU ka-ba-a si-ma-a
suk-na ya-si-sa
rimi-nin-ni-ma, ana-ku ___ , apil ___ sa
ilu-sa ___ u ilu-istari-su ___ .
ebbu ramanu nam-eme-sig u ummuqu si-mi-i
su-pi-ya
petu babu temu
amat a-kab-bu-u kima a-kab-bu-u lu-u
ma-ag-rat
sumu-ka ka-lis ina pi nisi ta-a-ab
anaku arad-ka elu
an-un-na-ki ti-i-ru u na-an-za-zu

PRAYER TO NABU & TESHMET
(ENGLISH)

NABU. TUTU. TESHMET – TASMIT(U).
NEBOS. MERCURIOS.
Scribe among the Gods,
Keeper of the Wisdom of the Gods,
Firstborn of MARDUK and SARPANIT.
NABU, Bearer of the Tablet of Destinies of
   the gods,
May my dreams [destiny] be filled with
   prosperity.
May my petitions fall on the ears of NABU &
   TASMIT (TESHMET).
Be favorable to me, I, __ son of __ , whose
   god is __ and whose goddess is __ .
Cleanse me of false knowledge, that I might
   be fit to call upon thee.
Open the Gates of your understanding to me.
Bless my mouth with true words to speak the
   prayers.
May the prayers rise from the lips of the
   people.
I am a servant of the Highest,
May the ANUNNAKI come forth and be
   established.

AN INVOCATION TO NABU

*Hero of BABYLON, prince and heir of Lord
    MARDUK,*
*NABU, Ruler of the Lands, the offspring of
    SARPANIT.*
*NABU, Caretaker of the Tablet of Destiny of
    the ANUNNAKI,*
*Spirit of the Gate of Lord NABU, swing wide
    the Gate.*
Lord of the Temples, Lord of the Mound
And the Tower of Nations,
Your name is in the mouth of the people.
*Son of MARDUK, Rightful heir of the
    MERKUR, hear me.*
*I, __, son of __, whose god is __, and whose
    goddess is __,*
*I am your servant, let me live and be perfect
    in your justice.*
*NABU, Spirit of BABYLON, remember, return,
    be established*
With the House of the ANUNNAKI,
And may they command mercy on Earth.
May my god stand at my right hand.
May my goddess stand at my left hand.
May the favorable guardian spirit be with me.
*NABU, firstborn of MARDUK, remember me
    and be merciful.*

AN INVOCATION TO TESHMET
(THE LADY TASMITU)

O Lady TASMITU (TESHMET)!
I __ , son of ___ and ___ ,
Whose god is ___ , whose goddess is ___ ,
In the evil of an eclipse of the Moon,
Which in ___ month on ___ day has taken
  place,
In the evil of the powers, of the portents,
Evil and not good, which are in my palace
  and my land,
I have turned towards thee! I have established
  thee!
Listen to the incantation!
Before NABU, thy spouse, the lord, the prince,
The firstborn son of the E.SAGILA, intercede
  for me!
May he hearken to my cry at the word of thy
  mouth;
May he remove my sighing;
May he learn of my supplication!
At his mighty word,
May god and goddess deal graciously
  with me!
May the sickness of my body be torn away;

May the groaning of my flesh be consumed!
May the consumption of my muscles be
removed!
May the poisons that are upon me be
loosened!
May the ban be torn away and the curse
consumed!
May the ANUNNAKI come forth and demand
justice!
At thy command, may mercy be established!
May god and king ordain favor
At thy mighty command that is not altered,
And thy true mercy that changes not,
O Lady TASMITU (TESHMET)!

A HYMN TO NABU

O Prince of Babylon, Heir-son of MARDUK,
O prudent ruler, offspring of SARPANIT.
O NABU, bearer of the Tablet of Destiny,
  who knows the fate of the gods,
High Priest of Babylon,
Director of the E.SAGILA,
Lord of the E.ZIDA,
Protector of Borsippa,
Beloved of E.A. (ENKI),
Granter of life;
Patron of Babylon,
Protector of the living god of inhabited hills,
  of the fortress of the people,
Lord of the temples, thy name is NABU;
  thy name is in the mouth of the people.
Son of the great Lord MARDUK,
In thy mouth is truth,
In thy illustrious name is truth,
By the command of thy great divinity,
May the favorable spirit and guardian
  be at my side.
May I bow in humility before thee,
  your faithful servant.

THURSDAY — JUPITER — MARDUK

The industrious and raw expansive power of Jupiter is placed at the height of most 'Olympian' pantheons (*Zeus* or similar). "Jupiter" comes from the Romans: *Dys Pater*, meaning "Father-God." This current commands outright worldly success and the magic of spirits: command of the hierarchies. Elder Gods originally attributed this position to ENLIL in Sumer. I personally heralded my father, MARDUK, into Enlilship of the "younger pantheon" in Babylon. Our tradition there, and in Egypt, was wholly based on him being the centralized figure. Invoke my father for his strength and power, as well as a petitioner to the Elder Gods.

He is exalted as the Master of Magicians, carrying the mysteries of my grandfather, ENKI, to Babylon, and bestowing the traditions upon me to relay as the archetypal High Priest of our tradition.

The original designation of Jupiter is 50, the number attributed first to ENLIL and later to MARDUK by the Babylonians, who first was given the number 10. The color of the current is purple, but also airy and fiery colors (yellow, orange, black). This energy is preferred by many leaders and law enforcing folk, lending to those who are pure to receive it, the power to command the material world.

PRAYER TO MARDUK & SARPANIT
(BABYLONIAN)

ilu-MAR.DUG. ilu-MAR.DUK. ilu-istari-
  ZARPANIT. ilu-silik-MULU.KHI DIL.GAN.
lugal arali, belu asipu
ilu-su BAB.ILI
ilu-SARPANIT(UM), belitu istari-su BAB.ILI
gasru u sapsu ina an-ki zi atwu
belu u belitu su BAB.ILI
maharu ramanu arua abnu-gesnu, abnu-uqnu
  u hurasu
dinu-ma ramanu lid-mi-ik
anaku ___ apil ___ sa ilu-su ___ u
  ilu-istar-su ___ .
lu-us-tam-mar ilu-ut-ka u atwu ramanu
  maharu karabu
petu babu temu – petu babu idu
ina ki-bi-ti-ka sir-ti lu-ub-lut lu-us-lim-ma
napsiti narbu ramanu ki-bi su su-sud ilani
  samu
anaku arad-ka elu
an-un-na-ki ti-i-ru u na-an-za-zu

PRAYER TO MARDUK & SARPANIT
(ENGLISH)

MARDUK. MERODACH. SARPANIT.
MULU-KHI. JUPITER.
Lord of the Lands, Master of Magicians,
God of Babylon.
SARPANIT, Lady of Babylon.
Mighty and powerful on earth and heaven are
*   your words.*
Lord and Lady of Babylon,
Accept my offerings of alabaster, lapis lazuli
*   and gold.*
Judge my life favorably,
I ___ , son of ____ , whose god is ____ , and
*   whose goddess is _____ .*
Make me fit to behold your divinity and teach
*   me to receive thy blessings.*
Open the Gates of your power to me.
Let me live. Let me be perfect.
Command greatness in my life as your
*   expansion permeates the gods of heaven.*
I am a servant of the Highest.
May the ANUNNAKI come forth and be
*   established.*

AN INVOCATION TO MARDUK

*MARDUK, Almighty, Powerful One of
   ASSUR,
Exalted, Noble-Blood, Firstborn of ENKI,
Almighty MARDUK, who causes the ITURA
   to rejoice,
Lord of ISAGILA, Aid to BABYLON, Lover of
   IZIDA,
Preserver of Life, Prince of IMATILLA,
   Renewer of Life,
Shadow over the Land, Protector of Foreign
   Lands,
Forever is MARDUK the Sovereign of
   Shrines,
Forever is MARDUK the Name in the mouth
   of the people.
I, __, son of __, whose god is __, and whose
   goddess is __,
Call to the Spirit of the MARDUK Gate to
   swing wide the Gate.
Almighty Lord MARDUK,
At your command the Earthborn remain alive,
At your command let me live and be perfect,
Let me behold your divinity.
What I will to be, let me obtain my wishes.
MARDUK, cause righteousness to come from
   my mouth,*

MARDUK, cause mercy to dwell in my heart,
Return to the Earth; establish the
   ANUNNAKI, command mercy.
May my God stand at my right hand.
May my Goddess stand at my left hand.
May my Lord who is favorable to the stars,
Stand firmly at my side,
Speak the Word of Command, to hear my
   prayer and show favor,
When I speak, let the words be powerful.
Almighty Lord MARDUK, come and
   command life.
BEL's Fires go with you, ENKI smile upon
   us all.
May the Good [Elder] Gods delight in your
   mercy.
May the Earth Gods [Deities] be favorable
   to thee and me.
Spirit of the Gate of MARDUK, open the
   gate to me.

Marduk, Great Lord,
Prince into whose hands the decrees of
   Heaven and the Underworld are entrusted;
May the servant who reveres you be well
   favored in your presence,
May he have a personal god and protecting
   angel beside him always.

AN INVOCATION TO SARPANIT
(TABLET-FRAGMENT)

Queen of ESAGILA, the palace of the gods,
  the House like a mountain
    (sar-rat I.SAG.ILA ikal ilani sa-du-u- . . .)
Lady of Babylon, the Shadow of lands!
    (Bi-lit Babili-ki su-lul ma-ta-a-ti)
Lady of the gods, who loves to give life,
    (ilu-Bilit ili sa bul-lu-ta i-ram-mu)
Who gives succor in sorrow and distress,
    (it-ti-rat ina puski u dannati)
The . . . one, who holds the hand of . . .
    (. . . -ma-li-tu sa-bi-ta kata-du na-as-ki)
Who supports the weak, who pours out seed,
    (i-pi-rat in-si sa-pi-kat ziru)
Who protects life, who gives offspring
  and seed,
    (na-si-rat napisti nadnat aplu u ziru)
Who bestows life, who takes away sighing,
  who accepts prayer,
    (ka-i-sat balatu li-kat un-ni-ni ma-hi-rat
    tas-lit)
Who has made the people, the whole of
  creation!
    (ba-na-at nisi gi-mir nab-ni-ta)

A HYMN TO SARPANIT

She is mighty, she is divine,
  She is exalted among the gods.
Zarpanit, brightest of the stars;
Shining Zarpanit, exalted and most high.
Among Goddesses, none are like her.
She accuses and intercedes;
She abases the rich and vindicates the cause
  of the lowly;
She overthrows the enemy, he who does not
  revere her godhead;
She delivers the captives;
She takes the hand of the fallen.
O, Zarpanit,
Let them tell of thy glory;
Let them exalt thy kingdom;
Let them speak of the prowess;
Let them glorify thy name.
Have mercy on me, thy servant, who blesses
  thee.
Take the hand of thy servant in need and
  suffering;
In disease and distress, give him life.
May he go forever in joy and delight.
May he tell of thy prowess to the people
  of the whole world.

FRIDAY — VENUS — ISHTAR

Most famous among energetic currents of these mysteries is Venusian. It is always dedicated to the "goddess of love and war." A determined goddess, she made her place among all ancient pantheons: whether *Isis*, *Aphrodite*, *Ashtoreth*... she is also known as the "goddess of witches," and celebrated in their rites.

In Babylon, by request of MARDUK, her political anger was appeased by being established as ISHTAR (Venus). When ISHTAR and MARDUK were not pair-bonded (as intended), each took it upon themselves to elevate and usurp their own positions of "reign" among our "younger pantheon."

The Venusian current (and that of Jupiter) are extremely powerful and actively raw energies. They are not always as obvious with their executions, such as you might find with the Sun or Mars, but they store mass amounts of energy for eventual release at the most "propitious" or favorable times. ISHTAR may be invoked to channel energies directed toward the acquisition of desires. (A wise one will be certain this is for their higher good first.) Her number is 15. Colors are green, yellow-green and white, and her elements are water and earth.

PRAYER TO ISHTAR & DUMUZI
(BABYLONIAN)

ilu-INANNA. ilu-istari-ISHTAR. ilu-DUMUZI.
  ilu-ISTAR.
belitu, martu-su ilu-NANNA-SIN sa karabu
  ina samu
ramu-su ilu-ANU, rabianu samu
namru-sat musi
lu-dub-gar-ra sat musi
li-iz-ziz ilu-istari-ya ina sumili-ya sutlumu
  karabu nissanu sabu u ilani
ilu-istari-ISHTAR u ilu-DUMUZI
rimi-nin-ni-ma, ana-ku ___ apil ___ sa
  ilu-sa ___ u ilu-istar-su ___
mesu-ya nigussu, anaku aga simtu maharu
  zi qistu
petu babu temu
li-iz-ziz ramanu manahtu-su zid
a-mat a-kab-bu-u kima a-kab-bu-u lu-u
  ma-ag-rat
is-ti-' nam-ri-ir-ri-ki lim-mi-ru samu kima
  nasaru sabu-su karabu
si-lim itti ya-a-tu-u anaku arad-ka elu
an-un-na-ki ti-i-ru u na-an-za-zu

PRAYER TO ISHTAR & DUMUZI
(ENGLISH)

INANNA. ISHTAR. DUMUZI.
ISTARI. VENUS.
Queen, Daughter of the Moon, who is blessed
by the heavens,
Beloved of ANU, the Command in Heaven,
Brightness of the Evening,
Huntress of the Night,
Do come to stand favorably at my side, grant
me the fruits of men and gods.
ISHTAR and DUMUZI,
Be favorable to me, I, ___ son of ___ , whose
god is ___ and whose goddess is ___ ,
Cleanse me of impurity make me a vessel fit to
receive your rewards.
Open the Gates of your understanding to me.
May my actions be true.
May the words I speak bring me to success.
May your light shining in the heavens be a
guide to all men you bless favorably.
Bless me, a servant of the Highest.
May the ANUNNAKI come forth and be
established.

AN INVOCATION TO ISHTAR

ISHTAR, Lady of the Sky,
Your throne rests in the bright starry heavens,
You who shines like the Sun-star
And who is given the Spirit of Venus,
You are powerful and exalted among nations
*   and the cosmos,*
Command the Light here on Earth,
Open wide the threshold of your Gate.
Goddess of goddesses have mercy upon me
And take pity on my sighs.
I call to thee: let there be good fortune and
*   prosperity in the lands.*
ISHTAR, Queen of the Horizon-Where-the-
*   Sun-Rises,*
I have quested for and behold your light,
Let also my brightness shine.
That which is on your right hand increase
The good fortune in the land,
And that which is in your left hand let it be
*   given your favor.*
I call to you to open the Gate in the name of
*   the Covenant sworn,*
I, __, son of __, whose god is __, and whose
*   goddess is __,*
I call to thee by the secrets of the gods,

*And in the name of the most holy Tablet of
    Destiny.*
*Let the words I speak be heard among the
    ANUNNAKI.*
*May the gods of the ANUNNAKI be favorable
    to thee and me.*
*Let your name be heard unto the distant
    nations of the world.*
*Gate of the Sphere of the Morning Star,
    open unto me.*

A HYMN TO INANNA-ISHTAR
(PRE-BABYLONIAN)

*Queen of the Heaven, Goddess of the
  Universe,
You are the holy one among women and men;
The one who walked in terrible chaos
  and brought life by the law of love;
And out of chaos brought us harmony;
And from chaos she has led us by the hand.
Woman of Women—Goddess who knows no
  equal;
She who decrees the destiny of the people,
Highest ruler of the world,
Sovereign of the Heavens,
Goddess of even those who live in Heaven.
With ISHTAR there is counsel and wisdom.
The fate of everything, she holds in her hand.
Joy comes from her every glance.
She is the power, the magnificence,
She is the deity who protects;
She is the spirit that guides, be it maiden or
  mother,
Women remember and call her name;
O Shinning One!*

SATURDAY — SATURN — NINURTA

Among planets, Saturn is traditionally the most dark and secretive, representing hidden power and the "*hidden key*" by which one may be released from the physical world of Gates and illusions. The Saturnalian current is a threshold to the Outer Ones that the secret societies and mystery schools have covertly sought through the ages. NINURTA represents Saturn in Mesopotamia—even in Babylon. He also reflects the dark secret of Babylon: He is the heir to Enlilship by one reckoning of the pantheon, a position MARDUK usurped for our reckoning of the pantheon in Babylon, for Mardukites.

In the Babylonian system, NINURTA is given a designation of 4. This indicates he is outside of the 'Olympian pantheon' of 'sky gods,' waiting to take his place, being heir of ENLIL with the number 50. Saturn energy is just as passively introspective as it is actively reflecting the outer world. These lessons demand a Seeker to confront dark, repressed, guilt-laden aspects of themselves, in order to ascend to a state of Self-honest wholeness. The elements of *air* and *earth* are both present in this current and the darker color spectrum is most resonant. Invoke NINURTA to aid in one's own path toward mastery in addition to giving recognition to correct the aspects that have kept the very system from achieving its own wholeness.

PRAYER TO NINURTA & BA'U
(BABYLONIAN)

ilu-NINURTA. ilu-NINIB. Ilu-istari-BA'U.
  ilu-ADAR.
siptu aplu gas-ru bukur ilu-ENLIL
su-bu-u man-za-za ina ilani rabuti siru
  rubu-su ilu-ENLIL u ilu-NINMAH
belu u beltu sihip same u erseti
ilu-NINIB u ilu-istari-BA'U
atwu karabu-ya kisalmahu
ana-ku ____ apil ____ sa ilu-su ____ u
  ilu-istar-su ____
an-ni pu-tur
sir-ti pu-sur
lu-us-tam-mar ilu-ut-ka u atwu ramanu
  lid-mi-ik
petu babu temu, anaku arad-ka elu
ilu-istar-BA'U, biltu sur-bu-tu, sela ummu
ilu-NINIB, nisirtu qarradu ilu-ENLIL
ki-bit narbu ramanu zi
si-lim itti ya-a-tu-u
sumu-ka ka-lis ina pi nisi ta-a-ab
an-un-na-ki ti-i-ru u na-an-za-zu

PRAYER TO NINURTA & BA'U
(ENGLISH)

NINURTA. NINIB. BA'U.
ADAR. SATURN.
Mighty firstborn son of ENLIL.
Great is your place among the gods, royal
  prince of ENLIL and NINMAH.
Lord and Lady of the heavenly abode,
NINIB and BA'U,
Speak favorably of me in your courts,
I, ___ , son of ___ , whose god is ____ , and
  whose goddess is ____ .
Absolve me of my sins.
Remove my iniquities.
Make me fit to call upon and receive your
  blessings.
Open the Gates of your Understanding to me,
  a servant of the Highest,
BA'U, Mighty Lady, merciful mother.
NINIB, hidden warrior of ENLIL.
Command greatness in my life.
Look upon me favorably.
May your name be in the mouth of the people.
May the ANUNNAKI return and be
  established.

AN INVOCATION TO NINIB-NINURTA

*Mighty son, first-born of ENLIL [BEL] in the
  Ancient of Days,*
*Powerful One, perfect offspring of the
  Heavens,*
*NINIB, clothed in the mantle of terror and
  Darkness,*
*Who walks the Path of the Dead passing the
  Gate of Death at will,*
*Mighty is the place of NINIB among the
  ANUNNAKI Gods.*
Exalted is your name in the E.KUR,
House of the ANUNNAKI on Earth,
*And your father ENLIL has made you the
  Lawmaker of the Gods.*
*In the name of the most ancient and sacred
  Covenant of the Gods,*
*And in the name of the secret and priceless
  Tablet of Destiny,*
*I, __, son of __, whose god is __, and whose
  goddess is __,*
*Call to the Gate of NINIB to open the
  judgment of mankind.*
*Gate of the Last Days, swing wide the doors
  to your power.*

*Come down and command, lead the people
    without a leader,*
*Hold the hand of the weak and exalt the one
    who is strong,*
*But grant both to pass through the Gate of the
    Spirit of NINIB.*
*NINIB, ANUNNAKI Prince, Dark Wanderer
    of Dark Places Between,*
*Hear my cries and take pity, show mercy to
    your servant of BABYLON.*
*Be favorable to me, take away my sins and
    remove my iniquities,*
*That I may come before my god and goddess
    in pure perfection.*
*May your name ever be praised among the
    words of the people.*

SUNDAY — THE SUN — SHAMMASH

The sun represents the brilliance and radiance of life on earth. It is the light that allows organic life to grow and it is also the manner in which time is divided, including a lifespan.

The sun also symbolizes expansive powerful energy and is often invoked for general success and well-being in this existence (and the next). The fiery nature of the star is called to "incinerate iniquities" and also to reveal darkness or lies: the revelation of truth.

Mistaken as monotheistic solar worship, the veneration of the sun is the celebration of life, and so annual festivals were marked by the path of the sun (at solstices and equinoxes). As a representative of "Heaven," the sun signifies the physical presence and watchful eye of "God" and is invoked to bring righteous judgment to critical situations.

In the Babylonian pantheon, the solar designation of 20 is given to SAMAS (*Shammash*) also known by the Sumerians as UTU. The colors of this energy current are bright (yellow, white, gold) and the dominant element is clearly fire or *starfire*. The prayer that follows, invokes SAMAS to come forth and be established as the supreme judge of the destinies of men on earth.

PRAYER TO SHAMMASH & AYA
(BABYLONIAN)

ilu-SHAMMASH. ilu-UTU. ilu-istari-AYA.
ilu-SAMAS. samsu.
anqullu u igigallu
dinu ilani
maru aplu ilu-NANNA-SIN
sapiru nam-simtu apitu
ilu-SAMAS u ilu-AYA
karabu danu simtu
metequ damaqu
la-kasadu immu kararu
ilu-SAMAS u ilu-AYA
si-lim itti ya-a-tu-u ___ , apil ___ , sa
  ilu-sa ___ , ilu-istar-su ___ .
napahu ramanu sir-tu
lu-ub-lut lu-us-lim-ma maharu nuru
enu atwu uznu ilu-ENLIL
petu babu temu
sumu-ka ka-lis ina pi nisi ta-a-ab
qibitu nig-silim ina ramanu napistu
ana-ku arad-ka elu
an-un-na-ki ti-i-ru u na-an-za-zu.

PRAYER TO SHAMMASH & AYA
(ENGLISH)

SHAMMASH. UTU. AYA.
SAMAS. SUN.
Fiery and Powerful One,
Judge among the gods,
Son of the Moon-god,
Overseer of the destinies of the lands.
SHAMMASH and AYA,
Be the favorable judges of my destiny.
May the path be prosperous.
Unequaled light of day,
SHAMMASH and AYA
Shine favorably on me, __ , son of __ ,
  whose god is __ and whose goddess is __ .
Incinerate my iniquities.
Make me perfect to behold your light.
Lord, who appeals to the ears of ENLIL,
Open the Gates of your understanding to me.
Permanent is your mighty word on earth.
May your unquestioned command dictate
  prosperity in my life.
I am a servant of the Highest,
May the ANUNNAKI return and be
  established.

AN INVOCATION TO SHAMMASH

*SAMAS [SHAMMASH], Judge of the
  ANUNNAKI Gods,*
*Lord of IGIGI, given the powers and forces
  of the Sun,*
SAMAS, Keeper of the Fiery Disk,
The Burning Disk, remember me.
*I, __, son of __, whose god is __, and whose
  goddess is __,*
*Call to the Spirit of the SAMAS Gate, open
  wide the Gate.*
*SAMAS, Spirit of the Sun, open the Gate of
  the Fiery Star.*
*I call to you from the Sphere of your sister,
  ISHTAR, hear my call.*
*In the name of the Ancient Covenant of the
  ANUNNAKI,*
*And in the name of the most holy Tablet
  of Destiny,*
I call to the Gate of the Sun to open wide.

SUPERNAL — E.A.–ENKI — NEPTUNE

ENKI assisted his brother ENLIL in developing the local universe, pre-Babylonian Sumer, and the organization of the local physical world. Later, ENKI or E.A. ("Whose House is Water") is given domain over physical manifestation and creation in the form of "magic." In Babylon we gave to him the name of EN.KI meaning "Lord of the Earth." In raising him to this position among the people it was much easier for his son, MARDUK, to be given a high station as well.

The elements *earth* and *air* are strong in this energetic current. ENKI is sometimes referred to as "Our Father" among *our* Race of Marduk. He is given charge of the *"Word of Power"* [called MAAT by the Egyptians] that charges the incantations of magic that breathe changes into the universe. These secrets were passed onto MARDUK and myself. They became the foundation of our traditions in Babylon and Egypt.

As a planetary power, ENKI is Neptune, the Greek 'Poseidon of the Deep.' His power is ancient and strong, knowing no boundaries in the universe. For a time he solely possessed all Anunnaki *Tablets of Destiny* and control of the 'Arts of Civilization' powering all magic in Mesopotamia and of the priests in Babylon.

PRAYER TO ENKI & DAMKINA
(BABYLONIAN)

ilu-E.A ilu-IA ilu-EN.KI
ilu-istari-NIN.KI ilu-istari-DAM.KI.NA
ilu-EN.KI samu-ya sa mesari eresti
ilu-istari-DAM.KI.NA sar-rat kal an-un-na-ki
  ilani la-tu
ilu-EN.KI u ilu-istari-DAM.KI.NA, sur-ba-ti
  ina ilani, la-u parsuki
rimi-nin-ni-ma anaku ___ apil ___ sa
  ilu-sa ___ u ilu-istari-sa ___
abu u ummu kispu
nabatu kabasu ramanu manahtu
rasanu-ya rigmu ina ramanu siptu
ki-bi-ma lis-si-mi zik-ri
amat a-kab-bu-u kima a-kab-bu-u lu-u
  ma-ag-rat
dinu-ma ramanu lid-mi-ik
lu-us-tam-mar ilu-ut-ka nabatu anaku
  arad-ka elu
an-un-na-ki ti-i-ru u na-an-za-zu
u emedu salimu menu u tes, enu zid katamu
  [AN.KI] sihip, same u eresti

PRAYER TO ENKI & DAMKINA
(ENGLISH)

EA. IA. ENKI.
NINKI. DAMKINA.
ENKI, Your name is the depths of the Earth.
DAMKINA, Queen among the Anunnaki Gods
ENKI and DAMKINA,You are great among
   the gods, Mighty is your command.
Be favorable to me ___ son of ___ whose
   god is ___ and whose goddess is ___ .
Father and Mother of Magic,
Shine upon my work.
Be the voice of my incantations.
Speak and let the Word be heard.
Let the Word I speak, when I speak it,
   be favorable.
Open the Gates of your understanding.
Judge my existence favorably.
Let your Divine Light shine through me,
   a servant of the Highest.
May the Anunnaki come forth and be
   established.
And may peace, love and unity, reign true
   throughout the Universe.

SUPERNAL — ENLIL (EL)
JUPITER (ELDER)

ENLIL is "Lord of the Command" – heir to *Anuship* in 'Heaven', position of 'God' in the local universe. This shift in power began the Judeo-Semitic age, when ENLIL appeared to the people of the "Holy Lands" as "Jehovah." It can be said that ENLIL is indeed the God of the Israelites and the Judeo-Christian and Islamic traditions.

The pantheon split. A duality between lineages of ENLIL and ENKI occurred on Earth and in Heaven. By one standard: ENLIL would be rightfully acknowledged as the power of *Anuship* (after ANU)—with his own heir, NINURTA as successor. Such was the original arrangement for the last age and for the "peace, love and unity to reign true in the Universe," it is essential that the perceptions of these traditions, in addition to their realizations in modern times, is carried in Self-Honesty.

Jupiter is the original current of ENLIL, though we observe MARDUK in Babylon, and the power to execute "*Anuship*" in the material world – an exercise of power in elemental domains of *air* and *fire* elements. Where ENKI is "Lord of the Earth," ENLIL is seen as "Lord of the Airs," the intermediary space bonding (between) the earth and the heavens.

PRAYER TO ENLIL & NINLIL
(BABYLONIAN)

ilu-ENLIL ilu-BEL
ilu-istari-NINLIL ilu-istari-BELTU
sumu-ya sa dug-ga
rigmu-ya dug-ga samu u erseti
ilu-ENLIL abu ilani
ilu-BEL-ENLIL u ilu-istari-BELITU-NINLIL
zi kima ramanu abu u ummu anaku___
*   apil ___ sa ilu-su ___ ilu-istari-su ___*
ka-ba-a sutlumu ramanu tehu u amaru
*   dingir-ya itti ilani*
sutlumu-lu manzazu-ya itti ilani masu
banu anaku aga zaku temu
petu babu temu
karabu ramanu manahtu u zaqtu napharu
lu-us-tam-mar ilu-ut-ka nabatu anaku
*   arad-ka elu*
qibitu narbu ina [An.Ki] sihip same u eresti
an-un-na-ki ti-i-ru u na-an-za-zu
u emedu salimu menu u tes enu zid katamu
*   [An.Ki] sihip same u eresti*

PRAYER TO ENLIL & NINLIL (ENGLISH)

ENLIL. BEL.
NINLIL. BELTU.
Your name is the command.
Your voice rules the Heavens and Earth.
ENLIL, Father of the Gods,
BEL-ENLIL and BELITU-NINLIL,
You are as a father and mother to me ____ ,
  son of ____ , whose god is ____ and whose
  goddess is ____ .
At your command, allow me to approach
  and behold your divinity among the gods.
Let not your place among the gods be
  forgotten.
Make me a vessel of clear understanding.
Open the Gates of your understanding to me.
Bless me in my workings and show me
  wholeness.
Let your divine light shine through me, a
  servant of the Highest.
Command greatness in the Universe.
May the Anunnaki come forth and be
  established,
 And may peace, love and unity reign true
  throughout the Universe.

THE GREAT HYMN TO ENLIL
(PRE-BABYLONIAN)

ENLIL,whose command is far reaching;
Whose "word" is lofty and holy;
Whose pronouncement is unchangeable;
Who decrees destinies unto the distant
  future. . .
The Gods of Earth bow down willingly before
  him;
The Heavenly gods who are on Earth
Humble themselves before him;
They stand faithfully, according to your
  instructions.
Lord who knows the destiny of The Land,
ENLIL, trustworthy in his calling;
ENLIL, who knows the destiny of Sumer,
ENLIL, trustworthy in his calling;
Father ENLIL,
Lord of all the lands;
Father ENLIL,
Lord of the Rightful Command;
Father ENLIL,
Shepherd of the Black-Headed Ones. . .
From the Mountain of Sunrise
To the Mountain of Sunset,
ENLIL, you are the Lord of the Airs.

SUPERNAL — ANU (AN) — URANUS

From the start of recorded history in Sumer, and cuneiform tablets kept by NABU *priest-scribes*, it is ANU who is given role of "Father in Heaven," All-Father of the gods. This is what He was to us all, the father of both ENLIL and ENKI. All members of the Anunnaki pantheon from both lineages are His children.

We consider the "*House of Anu*" as the "domain of Heaven," but also the name given to the local planet Uranus [UR-ANU]. His heavenly force has not always been immediately known on earth, and has been left to his heirs, ENLIL and ENKI, to command the cosmos in his stead.

ANU, the blessed Father of us all, shall ever remain in the mouth of the people—in the prayers. His legacy shall always remain on epic tablets and through the deeds of his children. His place in Heaven shall always be known to us, though it will be succeeded by another, as ANU leaves us more and more with only a Shade remaining—and a position in the heavens meant to be filled by ENLIL (and his successor, NINURTA).

With the dawning of the New Age comes another change in divinity. Let self-honest peace, love and unity reign true through the Universe when it does.

PRAYER TO ANU & ANTU
(BABYLONIAN)

ilu-ANU ilu-AN ilu-AN.NA ilu-istari-AN.TU
ilu-ANU abu ina samu
ilu-AN.NA samu-sa zi nigul sumu
daru-sa zi gitmalu-ya amatu
duru-sa zi dingir-ya edullu
zi biritu [an.sar] samu u [ki.sar] erseti
  sa-zi u'uru
madu ilani duru risatu zi mulammu
guhsu-ya gistaggu la urru
ilu-istaru-AN.TU ummu samu u nabalu
si-lim itti-ya a-tu-u
dingir hamdan ina samu lu-us-tam-mar
  itu-ut-ka u atwu ramanu lid-mi-ik
anaku ___ apil ___ sa ilu-su ___
  ilu-istar-su ___
anaku izuzzu wasru gudmu zi
anaku arad-ka-ya arad-ka elu
an-un-na-ki ahurru-ya ti-i-ru u na-an-za-zu

PRAYER TO ANU & ANTU
(ENGLISH)

ANU. AN. ANNA. Goddess, ANTU.
ANU, Father in Heaven.
Heaven is your everlasting name.
Eternal is your perfect Word.
Forever is your Divine Kingdom.
The domain of Heaven and Earth is yours
to command.
May the Great Gods ever rejoice in your
splendor.
May your Altar of Offering never be empty.
ANTU, Mother of the Sky and Land,
Be favorable to me.
Divine Union of Heaven, make me fit to call
upon and receive your blessings.
I, son of ___ whose god is ___ and whose
goddess is ___ ,
Stand humbly before thee in praise.
I am thy servant—a servant of the Highest.
May the Anunnaki, your children, come forth
and be established.

THE GREAT HYMN TO ANU

*ANU, King in Heaven, Eternal Prince of the
ANUNNAKI [gods],*
*Whose words are the rule over the Assembly
of the ANUNNAKI,*
*Lord of the unequaled Horned Crown [of
ANU],*
*You who can travel anywhere in the Universe
on a raging storm;*
*You who stands in the royal chamber admired
as king.*
*The ears of the IGIGI are directed to hear
your pure words,*
*The Assembly of ANUNNAKI gather around
thee in reverence.*
*At your command the ANUNNAKI [gods]
bow in salute;*
At your command the wind blows
And food and drink are abundant;
*At your command the angry demons turn back
to their habitations.*
*May all the gods of Heaven and Earth pray at
your Altar of Offering;*
*And may the Kings of Dragonblood on Earth
give you heavy tribute.*

May men pray to you daily and offer
  sacrifices and adoration.
May your heart be at rest and may you ever
  reign righteously.
To the city of __. show your abundant
  favor and grace.

A LITANY TO THE
ANUNNAKI ASSEMBLY
(HERMETIC)

Open to me, the Gates of Heaven.
Hear me, MAMMI, Mother among the
  ANUNNAKI [gods].
Hear me, ANU, Father of the ANUNNAKI
  [gods].
Hear me, ISTARA, Lady of AN [stars or
  "Heaven"].
Hear me, MARDUK, Lord of the Magicians
  and Priests on Earth.
Hear me, ENKI, Father of MARDUK and of
  Men on Earth.
Let me see the Stairway-to-the-Stars [Star-
  Gate or Ladder-of-Light],
Let me bare witness to your ascent and
  descent.
SARPANIT, Lady of the Shrine, Consort of
  MARDUK, lead me.
Open your mysteries, Mistress of the Spirits.
Open to me, the Primordial Heavens.
It is not I, but NABU, Herald of the Gods
  who calls to you.
It is not I, but GEB, Heir of the Gods in
  the Black Lands, who calls.

A SUPPLEMENTAL

APPENDIX

TO THE PRAYERS

*A collection of esoteric supplements
given in former editions.*

THE ENUMA ELIS

The Babylonian Cuneiform "Epic of Creation"
Mardukite Tablet-N Series and Tablet-F

TABLET I

When in the heights the Heavens had not been named; And the Earth had not yet been named; And the primeval APSU, who birthed them, And CHAOS, TIAMAT, The Ancient One, Mother to them all.

Their waters were as One and no field was formed, No marsh was to be seen; When of the gods none had been called into being, And none bore a name, and no destinies were ordained; Then were created the celestial gods in the midst of heaven, LAHMU and LAHAMU were called into being; And the Ages increased.

Then ANSAR and KISAR were created, And the god ANU then came forth who begat NUDIM-MUD [ENKI]. Abounding in all wisdom he had no rival. Thus the Great Gods were established. But TIAMAT and APSU were still in confusion, Troubled and in disorder. APSU was not diminished in might, and TIAMAT roared.

APSU, the begetter of the Great Gods, Cried unto MUMMU, his minister, And said: "MUMMU, thou minister that causes my spirit to rejoice,

Come with me to TIAMAT." So they went and consulted on a plan with regard to the gods, their sons.

APSU spoke: "Let me destroy their ways, let there be lamentation; And then let us lie down again in peace." When TIAMAT heard these words, she raged and cried aloud. She uttered a curse and unto APSU she asked: "What then shall we do?"

MUMMU answered giving counsel unto APSU, "Come, their way is strong, but you can destroy it; This day you shall have rest, by night shalt thou lie down in peace."

They banded themselves together; And at the side of TIAMAT they advanced; they were furious; They devised mischief without resting night and day. They prepared for battle, fuming and raging; They joined their forces and made weapons invincible; She spawned monster-serpents, sharp of tooth, and merciless of fang; With poison, instead of blood, she filled their bodies. Fierce monster-vipers she clothed with terror. With splendor she clothed them, she made them of lofty stature. Whoever beheld them, terror overcame him, Their bodies reared up and none could withstand their attack. She set up vipers and dragons, and the monster LAHAMU. And hurricanes, and raging hounds, and scorpion-men, And mighty tempests, and fish-men, and rams; They bore cruel weapons, without fear of the fight. Her commands were mighty, none could resist them; After this fashion she made eleven kinds of monsters.

Among the gods who were her sons, Inasmuch as he had given her support, She exalted KINGU; in their midst she raised him to power. To march before the forces, to lead the host, To give the battle-signal, to advance to the attack, To direct the battle, to control the fight, Unto him she entrusted, saying: "I have uttered the spell, In the assembly of the gods I have raised thee to power. The dominion over all the gods, I have entrusted unto thee. Be thou exalted, you are my chosen spouse, May your name be magnified among all ANUN-NAKI."

She gave him the Tablets of Destiny, on his breast she laid them, Saying: "Thy command shall not be in vain, And your decrees shall be established." Now KINGU, thus exalted, having received the power of ANU, Decreed the fate among the gods his sons, Saying: "Let the opening of your mouth quench the Fire-god; He who is exalted in the battle, let him display his might!"

TABLET II

TIAMAT made weighty her handiwork, Evil she wrought against the gods her children. To avenge APSU, TIAMAT planned evil, But how she had collected her forces, the god unto EA [ENKI] divulged. ENKI was grievously afflicted and he sat in sorrow.

The days went by, and his anger was appeased, And to the place of ANSAR his father he took his way. He went and, standing before ANSAR, his father, All that TIAMAT had plotted he repeated unto him, saying "TIAMAT, our mother hath conceived a hatred for us; With all her force she rages, full of wrath. All the gods have turned to her; With those, whom you created, they go to her side.

They have banded together and at the side of TIAMAT; And they advance; they are furious, They devise mischief without resting night and day. They prepare for battle, fuming and raging; They have joined their forces and are making war. TIAMAT, who formed all things, And made weapons invincible;

She hath spawned monster-serpents, Sharp of tooth, and merciless of fang. With poison, instead of blood, she hath filled their bodies. Fierce monster-vipers she hath clothed with terror; With splendor she has armed them; She has made them tall in stature. Whoever beholds them is overcome by terror, Their bodies rear up and none can withstand their attack.

She hath set up vipers, and dragons, and the monster LAHAMU; And hurricanes and raging hounds, and scorpion-men; And mighty tempests, and fish-men and rams; They bear cruel weapons, without fear of the fight. Her commands are mighty; none can resist them; After this fashion, huge of stature, She has made eleven kinds of monsters. Among the gods who are her sons, Inasmuch as he has given her support, She has exalted KINGU; In their midst she hath raised him to power.

To march before the forces, to lead the host, To give the battle-signal, to advance to the attack. To direct the battle, to control the fight, To him she has uttered the spell; She hath given to him the Tablets of Destiny, On his breast she laid them, saying: 'Thy command shall not be in vain; And your word shall be established.' "O my father, let not the word of thy lips be overcome, Let me go, that I may accomplish all that is in thy heart. I shall avenge."

TABLET III

ANSAR spoke to his minister: "O GAGA, thou minister who causes my spirit to rejoice; Unto LAHMU and LAHAMU I will send thee. Make ready for a feast, at a banquet let them sit, Let them eat bread, let them mix wine, That for MARDUK, the avenger, they may decree the fate. Go, GAGA, stand before them, And all that I tell thee, Repeat unto them, and say: 'ANSAR, your son, has sent me, The purpose of his heart he has made known unto me.

He said that TIAMAT, our mother, has conceived a hatred for us; With all her force she rages full of wrath. All the gods have turned to her, with those, whom you created; They go to her side. I sent ANU, but he could not withstand her; NUDIM-MUD [ENKI] was afraid and turned back. But MARDUK has set out, the champion of the gods, your son; To set out against TIAMAT his heart has called him. He opened his mouth and spake unto me, Saying: 'If I, your avenger, Conquer TIAMAT and give you life, appoint an assembly, make my fate preeminent and proclaim it so. In UP-SUKKINAKU seat yourself joyfully together; With my word in place I will decree fate. May whatsoever I do remain unaltered, May the word of my lips never be changed nor made of no avail.' Quickly decree for him the fate which you bestow So that he may go and fight your strong enemy."

GAGA went humbly before LAHMU and LA-HAMU, the gods, his fathers, and he kissed the ground at their feet. He humbled himself; then he stood up and spake unto them saying: "ANSAR, your son, has sent me; The purpose of his heart he hath made known unto me. He says that TIAMAT, our mother, hath conceived a hatred for us; With all her force she rages full of wrath." And he spoke the words of the tale. LAHMU and LAHAMU heard and cried aloud. All of the IGIGI wailed bitterly, saying: "We do not understand the deed of TIAMAT!"

Then did they collect and go—The Great Gods, all of them, the ANUNNAKI who decree fate. They entered in the House of ANSAR, kissed one another, They made ready for the feast, ate bread; And they mixed sesame-wine. They were wholly at ease, their spirit was exalted; Then for MARDUK, their avenger, they decreed the fate.

TABLET IV

The ANUNNAKI prepared for MARDUK a lordly chamber; Before his fathers as prince he took his place. "MARDUK, You are now chief among the Great Gods, Thy fate is unequaled, thy word is ANU. Your words shall be command, In your power shall it be to exalt and to abase. None among the gods shall transgress your boundary. Abundance, shall exist in thy sanctuary shrine, even if you lack offerings. MARDUK, you are our avenger! We give you sovereignty over the whole world. Sit down in might; be exalted in thy command. Your weapon shall never lose its power; it shall crush your enemy. Lord, spare the life of him that puts his trust in thee; But as for the god who began the rebellion, empty them of life."

The ANUNNAKI set out a garment and continued to speak to MARDUK: "May thy fate, O lord, be supreme among the gods; To destroy and to create; speak only the word; And your command shall be fulfilled. Command now that the garment vanish; And speak the word again and let the garment re-appear!" Then he spake the words and the garment vanished; Again he commanded it and the garment reappeared.

When the gods, his fathers, beheld the fulfillment of his word; They rejoiced, and they did homage unto him, saying, "Maerdechai! Maerdechai! MARDUK is king!" They bestowed upon him the scepter, the throne and the ring; They gave him invincible weaponry to overwhelm the enemy. "Go, and cut off the life of TIAMAT," they said. "And let the wind carry her blood into secret places."

MARDUK made ready the bow, his first choice in weapon; He slung a spear upon him. He raised the club in his right hand. The bow and the quiver he hung at his side. He set the FLAMING DISC in front of him; And with the flame he filled his body. He fashioned a net to enclose the inward parts of TIAMAT, He stationed the four winds so that nothing of her might escape; The South wind and the North wind and the East wind; And the West wind He created the evil wind; And the tempest, and the hurricane; And the fourfold wind; And the sevenfold wind, and the cyclone; And the wind which had no equal; He sent forth the winds which he had created, seven in total; To disturb the inward parts of TIAMAT.

Then MARDUK raised the thunderbolt, mounted the chariot; A storm unequaled for terror, and he harnessed four horses named DESTRUCTION, FEROCITY, TERROR, and SWIFTNESS; and foam came from their mouths; And they were mighty in battle, trained to trample underfoot.

With garments cloaked in terror and an over-powering brightness crowning his head, MARDUK set out toward the raging TIAMAT. Then the gods beheld him. And when the lord drew near, He gazed upon the inward parts of TIAMAT, He heard the muttering of KINGU, her spouse.

As MARDUK gazed, KINGU was troubled; The will of KINGU was destroyed and his motions ceased. And the gods, his helpers, who marched by his side, beheld their leader's fear and their sight was troubled. But TIAMAT did not turn her neck. She spit rebellious words.

MARDUK raised the thunderbolt; his mighty weapon, against TIAMAT, who was raging, and he called out: "You have become great as you have exalted yourself on high; And your heart has prompted you to call to battle. You have raised KINGU to be your spouse; You have chosen Evil and sinned against ANU and his decree. And against the gods, my fathers, you have dedicated yourself to a wicked plan. Let us face off now then in battle!"

When TIAMAT heard these words; She acted possessed and lost her sense of reason. She screamed wild, piercing cries; She trembled and shook to her very foundations. She recited an incantation, and cast a spell, And the gods of the battle cried out for their weapons.

Then TIAMAT and MARDUK advanced towards one another; The battle drew near.

Lord MARDUK spread out his net and caught her, And the evil wind that gathered behind him he let loose in her face when she opened her mouth fully. The terrible winds filled her belly; And her courage was taken from her; And her mouth opened wider.

MARDUK seized the spear and burst her belly; Severing her inward parts, he pierced her heart. He overcame her and cut off her life; He cast down her body and stood upon it. And after slaying TIAMAT, the leader of the ANCIENT ONES, The might was broken and her minions scattered. But they were surrounded, so that they could not escape.

MARDUK took them captive and broke their weapons; In the net they were caught and in the snare they sat down. And on the eleven monsters which she had filled with the power of striking terror, he brought them affliction; Their strength he stole and their opposition he trampled under his feet. From KINGU who he had conquered; He rightly took the Tablets of Destiny and sealed them with his seal, then hung them from his neck. Now after MARDUK had conquered and cast down his enemies; And had fully established ANSAR's triumph over the enemy; And had attained the purpose of NUDIMMUD [EA (ENKI)]; Over the captive gods he strengthened his position, and he returned to the conquered TIAMAT. With his merciless club he smashed her skull. He cut through the channels of her blood; And he made the North wind steal it away Outside in secret places between spaces. His fathers beheld, and rejoiced and were glad; Presents and gifts they brought unto him.

Then Lord MARDUK rested, gazing upon her dead body and devised a cunning plan. He split her up like a flat fish into two halves; One half of her he established a covering for heaven. Sealed with a GATE he stationed a WATCHER IAK SAKKAK and fixed him not to let her waters to ever come forth.

MARDUK passed through and surveyed the regions of Heaven; And over the Deep he set the dwelling of NUDIMMUD [ENKI]. And after measuring the structure of the Deep, he founded his Mansion, which was created likened to Heaven and he set down the fixed districts for ANU, EN-LIL and ENKI to reign.

TABLET V

MARDUK fixed the Star Gates of the Elder Gods;[7] And the stars he gave images as the stars of the Zodiac, which he fixed in place. He ordained the year and into sections he divided it; For the twelve months he fixed the stars.

He founded his Star Gate on NIBIRU[8] to fix them in zones; That none might rebel or go astray, he fixed the Star Gate of ENLIL[9] and IA [ENKI] alongside him. He opened great gates on both sides; He made strong gates on the left and on the right and in the midst thereof he fixed the zenith; He fixed the Star Gate for the Moon-god and decreed that he shine forth, trusting him with the night and to determine days; The first of the great gates he assigned to NANNA [SIN] and every month without ceasing he would be crowned, Saying: "At the beginning of the month, when you shine down upon the land, you command the trumpets of the six days of the moon, and on the seventh day you will divide the crown. On the

7 Presumably the formation of the local universe (solar system) of planets.
8 Interpreted by some scholars as the planet Jupiter.
9 ENLIL —listed as BEL in many versions.

fourteenth day you will stand opposite as half-moon. When the Sun-god of the foundation of heaven calls thee; On that the final day again you will stand as opposite. All shall go about the course I fix. You will be drawn near to judge the righteous and destroy the unrighteous. That is my decree and the covenant of the first gate."

The gods, his fathers, beheld the net which MARDUK had fashioned; They beheld his bow and how its work was accomplished. They praised the work which he had done and then ANU raised up and kissed the bow before the assembly of the gods. And thus he named the names of the bow, saying: "Long-wood shall be one name; And the second name shall be Dragonslayer, And its third name shall be the Bow-star, in heaven shall it remain as a sign to all."

Then ANU and MARDUK fixed a Star Gate for it too; And after the ANUNNAKI decreed the fates for the ANCIENT ONES, MARDUK set a throne in heaven for himself at ANU's right hand.

TABLET VI

The ANUNNAKI acclaimed him "First among the ELDER GODS." MARDUK heard the praises of the gods; His heart called to him to devise a cunning plan. He approached IA [ENKI] saying: "The Key to the GATE shall be ever hidden, except to my offspring. I will take my blood and with bone I will fashion a Race of Men, that they may keep watch over the GATE. And from the blood of KINGU I will create a race of men, that they will inhabit the Earth in service to the gods so that our shrines may be built and the temples filled. But I will alter the ways of the gods, and I will change their paths; Together shall they be oppressed and unto evil shall they no longer reign. I will bind the ELDER GODS to the WATCHTOWERS; let them keep watch over the GATE of ABSU and the GATE of TI.AM.TU and the GATE of KINGU. I bind the WATCHER IAK SAKKAK to the GATE with the Key known only to my Race. Let none enter that GATE; Since to invoke DEATH is to utter the final prayer."

The ANUNNAKI rejoiced and set their mansions in UPSUKKINAKU. When all this had been done, the Elders of the ANUNNAKI seated themselves around MARDUK and in their assembly they exalted him and named him FIFTY times, bestowing upon him the FIFTY powers of the gods.

THE TABLET OF THE FIFTY NAMES

1. The First Name is MARDUK-DUGGA-ANU, Son of the Sun, Lord of Lords, Master of Magicians; Most Radiant Among the Gods is he.

2. The Second Name is MARDUKKA, ANUN-NAKI Creator, Knower of the Secrets of MAR-

DUK, Time, Space & Creation [Geometry of the Universe].

3. The Third Name is ARRA-MARUTUKKU, Master of Protections and of the Gate to the AN-CIENT ONES; And to whom the people give praise as Protector of the City. Possessor of the ARRA-Star.

4. The Fourth Name is BARASHAKUSHU-BAALDURU, Worker of Miracles, with wide heart and strong sympathies.

5. The Fifth Name is LUGGAL-DIMMERANKI-BANUTUKKU, Commander of the Wind Demons, The Voice Heard Among the Gods.

6. The Sixth Name is NARI-LUGGAL-DIMM-ERANKI(A)-BAN-RABISHU, Watcher of the Star Gates of the IGIGI & ANUNNAKI; And who is named the Monitor of the Gods in their stations. Keeper of the Gates between worlds.

7. The Seventh Name is ASARU-LUDU-BAN-MASKIM, Wielder of the Flaming Sword, The Light of the Gods. Called for the safety and protection of the Gatekeeper.

8. The Eighth Name is NAMTILLAKU-BAN-UTUK-UKUT-UKKU, Master of the Death Gate and of Necromancy; And who is able to revive the Gods with a single prayer.

9. The Ninth Name is NAMRU-BAKA-KAL-

AMU, The Shining One who is Counselor of the Sciences. Called to increase the scientific knowledge of the Gatekeeper.

10. The Tenth Name is ASARU-BAALPRIKU, Creator of grains and plants, who knows no wasteland. Called to increase the vegetative and blooming growth.

11. The Eleventh Name is ASARU-ALIM-BAR-MARATU, who is revered for wisdom in the house of counsel; And who is looked to for peace when the Gods are unsettled. Called to aid in communication with the ANUNNAKI and to dispel deception.

12. The Twelfth Name is ASARU-ALIM-NUNA-BANA-TATU, The Mighty One who is the Light of the Father of the Gods; And who directs the decrees of ANU, ENLIL and ENKI/EA. Called to aid in the enforcement of law on Earth.

13. The Thirteenth Name is (NABU)-TUTU, He who created them anew, and should their wants be pure, then they are satisfied. Called to reveal the hidden gnosis within the Gatekeeper.

14. The Fourteenth Name is ZI-UKKINA-GIBIL-ANU, The life of the Assembly of the Gods; Who established for a bright place for the Gods in the heavens. Called to reveal the secrets of astrology and the celestial sphere.

15. The Fifteenth Name is ZI-AZAG-ZI-KU-

IGIGI-MAGAN-PA, Bringer of Purification, God of the Favoring Breeze, Carrier of Wealth & Abundance to the people.

16. The Sixteenth Name is AGAKU-AZAG-MASH-GARZANNA, Lord of the Pure Incantation, The Merciful One; And whose name is on the mouth of the Created Race. Called to bring life to elementaries and ward spirits.

17. The Seventeenth Name is TUKUMU-AZAG-MASH-SHAMMASHTI, Knower of the Incantation to destroy all evil ones. Called in the Maqlu Rite to dispel evil sorceries.

18. The Eighteenth Name is SAHG-ZU-MASH-SHANANNA, Founder of the Assembly of Gods and knows their heart; And whose name is heralded among the IGIGI. Called for aiding the Gatekeepers psychic development.

19. The Nineteenth Name is ZI-SI-MASH-IN-ANNA, Reconciler of enemies, who puts an end to anger; Bringer of Peace.

20. The Twentieth Name is SUH-RIM-MASH-SHA-NERGAL, Destroyer of wicked foes, who confuses their plans. May be sent to destroy the enemies of the Gatekeeper.

21. The Twenty-first Name is SUH-KUR-RIM-MASH-SHADAR, Who confounds the wicked foes in their places. May be sent to destroy the unknown enemies of the Gatekeeper.

22. The Twenty-second Name is ZAH-RIM-MASH-SHAG-ARANNU, Lord of Lightning, A warrior among warriors. May be raised against entire armies of men.

23. The Twenty-third Name is ZAH-KUR-RIM-MASH-TI-SHADDU, Destroyer of the Enemy in battle; Who slays in a most unnatural fashion.

24. The Twenty-fourth Name is ENBILULU-MASH-SHA-NEBU, Knower of the secrets of water and of secret places for grazing. Called to bestow the secrets of dowsing and aid irrigation.

25. The Twenty-fifth Name is EPADUN-E-YUNGINA-KANPA, Lord of Irrigation, who sprinkles water in the heavens and on Earth. As the previous, also the secrets of Sacred Geometry.

26. The Twenty-sixth Name is ENBI-LU-LU-GUGAL-AGGA, Lord of growth and cultivation, who raises the grains to maturity; And some have said is a face of ENKI.

27. The Twenty-seventh Name is HEGAL-BURDISHU, Master of farming and the plentiful harvest; And who provides for the people's consumption. May also be called to aid in personal fertility.

28. The Twenty-eighth Name is SIRSIR-APIRI-KUBAB-ADAZU-ZU-KANPA, The domination of TIAMAT by the power of the Net. Called for mastery of the Serpent and the Kundalini.

29. The Twenty-ninth Name is MAL-AHK-BACH-ACHA-DUGGA, Lord of bravery and courage, Rider of the Ancient Worm. Summoned for courage, bravery and self-confidence.

30. The Thirtieth Name is GIL-AGGA-BAAL, Furnisher of the life-giving seed, Beloved (betrothed) consort to INANNA-ISHTAR. Called for women who desire pregnancy.

31. The Thirty-first Name is GILMA-AKKA-BAAL, Mighty One and Divine Architect of the temples. Possesses secrets concerning the Geometry of the Universe.

32. The Thirty-second Name is AGILMA-MASH-SHAY-E-GURRA, Maker of Rain Clouds to nourish the fields of the Earth. Called forth in times of drought.

33. The Thirty-third Name is ZULUM-MU-AB-BA-BAAL, Giver of excellent counsel and power in all businesses; And Destroyer of the wicked foe, maintaining goodness and order.

34. The Thirty-fourth Name is MUMMU, Creator of the Universe from the flesh of TI.AM.TU. Keeper of the Four Watchtower Gates to the Outside.

35. The Thirty-fifth Name is ZU-MUL-IL-MAR-AN-DARA-BAAL; The heavens have none equal in strength and vitality. Called forth to aid in healing rituals and rites.

36. The Thirty-sixth Name is AGISKUL-AG-NI-BAAL-LUGAL-ABDUBAR, Who sealed the ANCIENT ONES in the abyss. Called by the piously righteous for strength and vigor.

37. The Thirty-seventh Name is PAGALGUEN-NA-ARRA-BA-BAAL, Possessor of Infinite Intelligence, preeminent among the Gods. Offers wisdom in oracles and divination.

38. The Thirty-eighth Name is LUGAL-DUR-MAH-ARATA-AGAR-BAAL, King of the gods, Lord of Rulers [*durmah*]. Aids the Gatekeeper in developing all mystic powers.

39. The Thirty-ninth Name is ARRA-ADU-NUNA-ARAMAN-GI, Counselor of ENKI/EA, who created the Gods, his fathers; And whose princely ways no other God can equal. Called during (self)-initiations to aid you through the Gates.

40. The Fortieth Name is DUL-AZAG-DUMU-DUKU-ARATA-GIGI, Possessor of the secret knowledge and the wand of Lapis Lazuli. Can reveal untold marvels of the cosmos to the Gatekeeper.

41. The Forty-first Name is LUGAL-AB-BA-BAAL-DIKU, Eldest of the Elder Ones, and pure is his dwelling among them. Aids the Gatekeeper in acquiring "Self-Honesty."

42. The Forty-second Name is LUGALDUL-AZAGA-ZI-KUR, Knower of the secrets of the spirits of wind and star. Offers the Gatekeeper secrets to command the spirits.

43. The Forty-third Name is IR-KINGU-BAR-E-RIMU, Holding the capture of KINGU, supreme is his might. Keeper of the Blood(Birth)-Rights.

44. The Forty-fourth Name is KI-EN-MA-EN-GAIGAI, Supreme Judge of the ANUNNAKI, at whose name the gods quake. To be called when no other spirit will arrive.

45. The Forty-fifth Name is E-ZIS-KUR-NEN-IGEGAI, Knows the lifespan of all things; And who fixed the Created Race's life at 120 years.

46. The Forty-sixth Name is GIBIL-GIRRA-BAAL-AGNI-TARRA, Lord of the sacred fire and the forge, creator of the Sword. Also possesses the secrets of the "fiery passions."

47. The Forty-seventh Name is ADDU-KAKO-DAMMU, Raiser of storms that blanket the skies of Heaven.

48. The Forty-eighth Name is ASH-ARRU-BAX-TAN-DABAL, Keeper of time, the secrets of the past and future. May be summoned to aid acts of divination.

49. The Forty-ninth Name is The STAR, let NE-BIRU be his name; He who forced his way through the midst of TIAMAT, May he hold the ALPHA and the OMEGA in his hands. Summoned to discern the Destiny of the Universe.

50. The Fiftieth Name is FIFTY and NINNU-AM-GASHDIG, The Judger of Judges, Determiner of the laws of the Realm. The Patron of the Dragonblood Kings of Earth.

THE MARDUK TABLET APOCRYPHA

The Forty-ninth Name is the STAR, that which shines in the heavens. May he hold the ALPHA and the OMEGA in his hands; And may all pay homage unto him, saying: "He who forced his way through the midst of TI.AM.TU without resting, Let NIBIRU be his name – The Seizer of the Crossings[10] that causes the stars of heaven to uphold their paths. He comes as a shepherd to the gods who are like sheep. In the future of mankind at the End of Days, may this be heard without ceasing; may it hold sway forever! Since MARDUK created the realm of heaven and fashioned the firm earth, He is forever the Lord of this World."

ENLIL listened. ENKI heard and rejoiced. All of the Spirits of Heaven waited. ENLIL gave to MARDUK his name and title BEL. ENKI gave to MARDUK his name and title EA and said: "The binding of all my decrees, let MARDUK now control. All of my commands, shall he make known."

The Fiftieth Name is FIFTY and NINNU-AM-GASHDIG, The Judger of Judges, Determiner of the laws of the Realm. By the name FIFTY did the ANUNNAKI then proclaim MARDUK's "Fifty

---

10 NIBIRU —given as "*Nebiru*" in some translations, meaning literally "Crossings" such as "in or around a midsection" or "midway around."

Names." The ANUNNAKI made his path preeminent.

Let the Fifty Names of MARDUK be held in remembrance to all; And let the leaders proclaim them; Let the wise gather to consider them together; Let the father repeat them and teach them to his son; Let them be in the ears of the priest and the shepherd. Let all men rejoice in MARDUK, the Lord of the gods,

That he may cause the land, his Earth, to be prosperous; And that he himself may enjoy prosperity! His word holds and his command is unaltered; No utterance from his mouth goes unnoticed. His gaze is of anger and turns his back to none; No god can withstand his wrath. And yet, wide is his heart and broad is his compassion; The sinner and evil-doer in his presence weep for themselves and pray for forgiveness.

DICTIONARY OF ANUNNAKI GODS

ADAD {10}—The youngest son of ENLIL that becomes the national patron deity to the *Hittites* (called HADAD or TESHUB); possibly also recognized as BAAL HADAD in a *Hittite* version of the Supernal Trinity that is elevated to a chief god position in the same manner that MARDUK is raised in *Babylon*. As a storm god in the Anunnaki pantheon, ADAD is represented by thunder, lightning and torrents. According to Hittite records, succession of hierarchical kingship passes from ALALU to ANU to KUMARBI (ENLIL) and then BA'AL HADAD (TESHUB). In the Enki'ite (Mardukite) Babylonian system he is named ISHKUR and granted the position of "*Inspector of the Cosmos*" by ENKI.

ALALU ["*Father of the Gods*"]—The figure maintaining 'kingship' in the 'heavens' prior to ANU. An ancient *Hittite (Hurrian)* tablet cycle titled ALALU & ANU or "*Kingship in Heaven*" describes a conflict between the two for the seat of 'kingship' in the 'heavens'. The Mardukite *Tablet-K* series reprinted in "*The Anunnaki Bible*" explains: Formerly in the Ancient of Days, ALULU was reigning in heaven; and for nine *sars* did he rule the skies, but not well did he reign. Then in the ninth *sar* of his reign, ANU defeated ALULU. ALULU descended from heaven and ruled the dark-hued earth. ANU gave fight and defeated

ALULU and kingship was lowered from heaven to earth by decree of ANU.

ALULU *see* ALALU

ASAR(I)LUHI *see* MARDUK

AMARUTU *see* MARDUK

AN/ANSAR *see* ANU

ANTU {55} ["*Life of Heaven*"]—The official half-sister (by a different mother) and spouse (consort) of ANU. ANTU and ANU beget ENLIL. In archaic pre-*Sumerian* lore, ANTU is espoused to the archaic AN.

ANUNITUM *see* INANNA

ANU {60} ["*Heavenly One*"]—In the *Sumerian* Anunnaki patheon, ANU is the supreme "*All-Father*" of the pantheon; father to ENLIL by official spouse ANTU, and the father of ENKI & NINHURSAG (by other wives). Called AN in pre-*Babylonian* times and ANU by the *Babylonians*, a being whose family resides on, or emerged from the 'place of crossings' (*Nibiru*). Few of the incantation tablets (or 'prayers') invoke the powers of ANU directly, since the "heavenly force" was perceived as too vast to be channeled in its raw state, and to degrade it to anything more accessible would be to compromise the nature of what is being represented by this figure.

ANZU [*"Knower of Heaven"*]—An obscure bird-like beast/monster of an unclear nature. The ANZU or ZU usually refers to a "heavenly bird" or thunderbird that appears in an archaic tab-let cycle stealing the *'Tablets of Destiny"* from EN-LIL, disrupting the DUR-AN-KI ('Bond-Heav-en-Earth') "stargate." It is possible that this half-man, half-bird, sometimes called AZAG, was a ge-netically engineered storm-god or artificially intel-ligent messenger being of ENLIL that turned "evil."

ARURU—The sister of ENLIL, alias NINTU, who is the *Babylonian* title for the 'mother-god-dess' known in *Sumerian* as NINMAH or NIN-HURSAG. In the Babylonian ethnocentric epics, she assists MARDUK in creating the human race (or *'Race of Marduk'*), however, in the *Enuma Elis*, it is "blood" of KINGU that is used. Other *Sumerian* versions say the "blood" or "essence" of some other 'slain' god is used for this.

AYA [*"Dawn"*]—The official spouse (consort) of SAMAS in *Akkadian*; named SHERIDA in *Sumerian*.

AZAG *see* ANZU

BAU [*"To Accompany"*]—A daughter of ANU, who is the official spouse (consort) to NINURTA in the pre-*Babylonian* (*Sumerian*) pantheon. Her names GULA (*"Big One"*) and BAU (the sound a dog makes) are, perhaps idioms about her size/appearance. She remains a goddess in the *Babylonian* pantheon of healing (as NINTI-NUGGA).

BEL *see* EL

BUZUR *see* ENKI

DAMKINA *see* NINKI

DAMUZU *see* DUMUZI

DUMUZI [*"Son Who is Life"*]—Youngest son of ENKI and DUTTUR (a concubine of ENKI) who is the betrothed spouse (consort) to INANNA (ISHTAR) after MARDUK declines the tradition of espousing INANNA. DAMUZI is a shepherd god (as opposed to a grain deity), known as TAMMUZ in the Semitic languages. In the *Sumerian* version of the descent-cycle, INANNA descends to the *Underworld* in hopes of being its queen. When captured, she becomes a prisoner of her sister ERESHKIGAL and leaves to find someone to take her place. Upon returning to ERECH, she finds that DUMUZI has been celebrating his ascent to her throne and is not mourning for her death. Enraged, she immediately hands him over to the 'demons' of the *Underworld*. Later versions of this cycle depict the god MARDUK as somehow responsible for the death of DUMUZI and INANNA (ISHTAR) descends to the *Underworld* to release him.

EA *see* ENKI

EL—A Semitic form of the Akkadian (*Babyloni-an*) ILU or ILI, meaning '*Lofty Ones*', '*High Ones*' or '*Great Gods*'; the plural form being ILANI (or ELANI in *European Elvish-Faerie* lore), with a Semitic plural equivalent "*Elohim*", meaning liter-ally 'gods' but often used to denote the 'One God' in the Judeo-Christian *Old Testament* (which is, it-self, rooted strongly in Mesopotamian traditions). EL or BEL is also used to denote the 'Lord of the Earth-Space', or else 'ENLIL-SHIP', a position attributed not only to ENLIL (in the *Enlilite Sumerian* tradition) but also to NINURTA, MAR-DUK and even other patron deities by localized Middle Eastern cults. Later Semitic use of EL as a suffix (e.g., Micha*el*, Gabri*el*, etc.) matches the prefix use of the ILU sign in cuneiform, meaning "*Of God.*" In cuneiform, the sign is a "cross" and in later religious scriptures and rites, the literary tradition remained to place a cross before a *Divine* or saint name.

ELLIL *see* ENLIL

ENKI {40} "*Lord of the Earth*"—also known as E.A. ["*Whose Home is Water*"], firstborn son of ANU (but not the official heir), half-brother to ENLIL (heir of ANU). Also called NUDIMMUD (or PTAH in *Egypt*) meaning: "*The Fashioner*" (or "*Grand Designer*"). ENKI is the Chief scientist of the Anunnaki, taking up residence in *Eridu*, near the *Persian Gulf* and also in *Africa* (particularly *Egypt*). ENKI is father of MARDUK, begot with NINKI (DAMKINA) and is representative of the planet Neptune in the local Anunnaki 'world order'. ENKI is given control of the '*Waters of Life*' on Earth. He seeks to save his own ('*Mardukite*') legacy during the deluge and then is responsible for programing the arts and sciences of civilization into humanity. In later *Enlilite*-derived Judeo-Christian interpretations, ENKI becomes demonized as 'Satan'.

ENLIL {50} "*Lord of Air-Space*"—The official heir-son of ANU, '*Lord of the Command*' on Earth, revered as the '*God*' of Earth by Enlilite *Sumerians* and later derived Semitic (Hebrew) tradtions. ENLIL begets his own heir, NINURTA, by his half-sister NINHURSAG, but espouses SUD, renamed NINLIL and begets NANNA. In the pre-*Babylonian* paradigm, ENLIL is the Jupiter position in the pantheon that is later usurped by MARDUK. *Sumerian* tradition observes ENLIL as the 'Father' to the Anunnaki pantheon, much in the same way that ENKI is revered by the *Mardukites*. Prominent descendents of ENLIL include: NANNA, SAMAS, INANNA and NERGAL in addition to NINURTA.

ENSAG *see* NABU

ENSHAG *see* NABU

ERESHKIGAL – ["*Mistress of the Great Below*"] The Queen of the *Great Lands* in the *Sumerian* tradition, sister of INANNA-ISHTAR, granddaughter of ENLIL and spouse to NERGAL.

ERRA *see* NERGAL

GANZIR — The gatekeeper to the underworld 'Kingdom of Shadows.' The '*Gate of Ganzir*' is often confused with the '*Gate to the Abyss*' or the '*Gate to the Outside*', but instead it is a portal into the Anunnaki-controlled *Underworld*, the '*Shadowlands*' or twilight world within the domain of ERESHKIGAL, who rules this 'land of the dead'. Quoting a modern grimoire of Babylonian occultism, the "necromantic art, by which is it desirous to speak with the phantom of someone dead, and perhaps dwelling in the ABSU [*Abyss*] and thereby a servant of ERESHKIGAL... it is no less than the opening of the *Gate of Ganzir.*"

GIBIL ["*He Who Has Fire*"]—The companion of the flame, a descendent of ENKI who uses fire to conduct alchemy and other feats of "*fire power.*"

GIRRA—The "servant", "power" or "fire" of the 'great god'; the *Sumerian* fire-god or essence or force of a fire-god named GIBIL.

GULA *see* BAU

HADAD *see* ADAD

ILLIL *see* ENLIL

ILU *see* EL

IMDUGUD *see* ANZU

INANNA {15} ["*Lady of Heaven*"]—The *Sumerian* goddess of "passion", both 'love' and 'war', and patron of URUK, begot by NANNA and NINGAL; originally betrothed to MARDUK, she then changes her consort choice to DUMUZI. Her prowess and determination secured her a place in all ancient pantheons; being the "*Goddess of One-Thousand Names,*" titled ISHTAR in *Babylon*. INANNA (ISHTAR) is the spirit of Venus, whose day is Friday and with an essence found in copper. Her colors are green and white, significant to her domain of fertility and growth. She offers her magicians the skills in love and visions of beauty.

IRRA *see* NERGAL

ISHKUR *see* ADAD

ISHTAR *see* INANNA

KUR *see* TIAMAT

MAMMI *see* NINHURSAG

MARDUK {10/(50)} "*Son of God*"—The supreme champion of the IGIGI during the pre-

Sumerian era of the Anunnaki; heir-son of ENKI, he becomes the patron of *Babylon* and the 'Mardukite' tradition reigning for the *Age of Aries* in Mesopotamia. All tablet cycles making reference to MARDUK are purely *Babylonian* or from a direct later source, as he does not appear in any significant pre-Babylonian cuneiform tablet cycles yet unearthed. When mentioned briefly as the son of ENKI, working in *Eridu*, he is named AS-ARLUHI, becoming the patron Anunnaki "deity" of magic or 'Master of Magicians'after having inherited the craft from his father. The blatant industrious and expansive power represented by MARDUK in his ascent up the pantheon (as observed in *Babylon*) is typified by the planet Jupiter (ENLIL, by *Sumerian* standards). His color is purple.

MERIDUG *see* MARDUK

MERODACH *see* MARDUK

NABAK *see* NABU

NABIH *see* NABU

NABU {12} ["*Prophet*"]—The official post-*Sumerian* secretary of the Anunnaki, part-divine earth born heir-son of MARDUK and messenger-herald and spokesperson of the '*Mardukite*' tradition, the national cult of *Babylon* devised by NABU who assisted his father in the redevelopment of the Anunnaki paradigm (as seen in the

'*Mardukite*' religion of *Babylon* replacing the previously observed *'Enlilite'* world order of the *Sumerians*). Creating the concept of 'history' and 'propaganda', NABU gives the 'stylus' to humanity (and launches a group of scribe-priests (specially taught writing and rhetoric) to catalog the natures, identities, history and decrees (decisions) of the Anunnaki Assembly (gods) and their relationship with each other and the human ("mortal") world, thereby creating not only the first public 'religion', but the first 'mythology' (a religion rooted in literary and oral legacies of human relationships and encounters with the divine) and the systems that were able to later result (most of which are still functioning as part of 'normal' everyday life in contemporary society). NABU is the archetypal *'High Priest'* (ENSAG) of the first religion (dedicated to MARDUK) and practiced by priests who preserve the craft of ENKI in *Eridu* with science and 'magic' of the gods to power and sustain the prosperous longevity of *Babylon*.

NAMRASIT *see* NANNA

NAMMTAR *see* NAMTAR

NAMMU *see* TIAMAT

NAMTAR ["*Fate Maker*"]—The 'Black Magician', vizier of ERESHKIGAL in the *Underworld*, also likened to the *Assyrian (Chaldean)* plague-god NAMTARU (also the *Akkadian* word for pest-

ilence"). From a ritual text given in *Liber 9* (Tab-
let-Q in *The Complete Anunnaki Bible*), the priest
is to make an image of the affected (sick) person
in dough [flour], so as to force the 'plague-god'
that afflicts the person to come away from the
body and go into the image. The ancient tablets list
the name of the plague-god as NAMTARU, and
in other places as URA and even URAS (in
Egypt). In the 'Descent'-cycle, ERESHKIGAL
summoned NAMMTAR, the Black Magician, saying these words as she spoke to him: 'Go, NAM-
MTAR, imprison her [INANNA] in Darkness, in
my castle! Release against her the Seven Anunnaki
Judges! Release against her the Demons of the
Deep...' Then, finally, the representation of a 'de-
mon', like the plague-god NAMTARU, was not intended for 'worship' or 'veneration' (as we might
see glorified among today's misguided attempts toward 'dark paths') as a deity. Such statuary typically was constructed only to be 'ceremonially' an-
nihilated or buried as a 'ward' against what the
statue (deity) represented.

NAMTARU *see* NAMTAR

NANNA {30}—The official lunar deity of the Enlilite *Sumerian* Anunnaki pantheon, the moon-god,
reigning with his feminine lunar consort, NIN-
GAL. An Anunnaki designation of 30 is significant
to the approximate number of days in a month;
whereby the original Sumerian calendar consists

of twelve cycles of 30 days for a 360 day year (and the reason a circle is divided into 360 degrees). NANNA and NINGAL begot the twins: INANNA and SAMAS; mythographically, the *moon* gave birth to the *sun* and V*enus* is a twin-star to the *sun*. To the ancient, the moon was the 'sun-at-night'. It illuminated the pathway for travelers and kept 'watch' as the people slept. Just as the sun is invoked to grant judgments of the daytime [see SAMAS], the moon is given domain of the night and *dreamscapes* (including the 'astral plane'). The day, "Monday", is obviously named after the moon, and is likewise sacred. The essence and color of silver is usually corresponded.

NANNAR *see* NANNA

NEBO *see* NABU

NERGAL {8}—The official spouse (consort) of ERESHKIGAL ('*Queen of the Underworld*'). NERGAL corresponds to the symbol and energetic current of *Mars,* with a fiery and destructive nature commemorated in the *Babylonian* epithet ERRA ("*Annihilator*"). The vitality and raw power of *Mars* (ruling Tuesday) is evident in the essences: iron and blood.

NINAGAL—An epithet meaning "*Prince of the Great Waters*," the name appears for a son of ENKI, who in the *Ziusurda* (*Atra-Asis*) cycle is selected by ENKI to navigate the archetypal "ark" sea-craft during the Great Flood.

NINANNA *see* INANNA

NINGAL {25} ["*Great Lady*"]—The daughter of ENKI; espoused (consort) to NANNA (SIN) and the mother of INANNA (ISHTAR) and SAMAS.

NINGISHZIDA—The 'Lord of the Tree of Life', a son of ENKI and brother to MARDUK, known as *Hermes* and *Thoth-the-Elder* (or TUTU) in a time before NABU. He is a geneticist, trained under ENKI in the arts of life engineering (and reality engineering) that was later taught by NABU (*Thoth-the-Younger* or TUTU) and it evolved into the mystical school of 'Hermetics' (or 'Hermeticism'). Having lost in the 'Pyramid Wars' (c. 3400 B.C. to 3150 B.C.) against MARDUK (RA) and not participating in the pro-MARDUK revolution of ENKI's lineage, NINGISHZIDA establishes his own realm in South America, known by the indigenous people and tradition as QUETZAL-COATL, the 'feather-ed serpent' (literally 'plumed serpent').

NINHARSAG *see* NINHURSAG

NINHURSAG {5}—The chief Anunnaki physician, the mother of NINURTA by ENLIL; a half-sister to ENLIL and ENKI by ANU. In an attempt to produce a royal heir or his own, ENKI even courts her at one time. She is not espoused to any of the pantheon, but instead serves the role of 'birth-goddess' and 'midwife' to the birth and raising of the Anunnaki children (of the Younger Generation), carrying names like MAMMI (*"Mother"*) and NINTI (*"Lady of Life"*). When attempting to relieve the toiling of the IGIGI faction of the Anunnaki, ENKI seeks out NINHURSAG to assist in the 'creation' of the 'human' race. Her response, being: 'If ENKI will provide for me the clay, then I will make the creation'. In this antropogenetic cycle, she mixes the clay with the flesh and blood of 'Awmelu' (presumed to be a slain deity). In other versions, the 'essence' is more clearly semen and/or other genetic material. Cuneiform tablet records indicate that six different attempts are made before the '*Adamu*' (the seventh) is fashioned.

NINIB *see* NINURTA

NINKI {35} [*"Lady of the Earth"*]—The official spouse (consort) of ENKI, also known as DAMKINA [*"Lady Who Came to Earth"*]. NINKI is the daughter of ALALU (the 'heavenly' king prior to ANU) and the the mother of MARDUK.

NINLIL {45} *"Lady of Air-Space"*—The official spouse (consort) of ENLIL, also known with the epithet SUD ("nurse"). The background to the relationship between ENLIL and NINLIL is not commonly found in the typical cuneiform tablet cycles. Naturally, the lore is *not* Mardukite or

Babylonian in origin and does not appear in the tablet catalogue or commentary of (modern) Mardukite Core anthologies. The cycle is sometimes referred to as *"Enlil's Banishment to the Underworld."*

NINMAH *see* NINHURSAG

NINSHUBAR *see* NINSHUBUR

NINSHUBUR [*"Lady of the East"*]—Personal assistant (Mercury), second-in-command to the goddess INANNA (ISHTAR). She does not take a consort and there is an alluded love-relationship between her and INANNA (ISHTAR).

NINSUBAR *see* NINSHUBUR

NINTI *see* NINHURSAG

NINTINUGGA *see* BAU

NINTU *see* ARURU

NINURTA {4/(50)} *"Lord of the South Wind"*— The official heir-son of ENLIL, born of ENLIL and NINMAH, espoused to BAU. NINURTA represents the current of Saturn in the Mardukite paradigm, representative both of "hidden power" and "hidden secrets" (an idiom for the dark power and secrets behind the origins and legacy of *Babylon*). In the Enlilite *Sumerian* worldview, NINURTA (called NINIB in *Babylonian*) is the

Enlil-in-waiting, a position usurped by MARDUK proper for the *Age of Aries*. As Enlilship is typically symbolized by 'dragon-slaying', the same motif present in the elevation of MARDUK in *Babylon* rivaling the dragon-queen TIAMAT can be seen in the older *Sumerian* cycles where the prowess of NINURTA is shown in his ability to fight the mighty dragon KUR. His colors are black and violet and his essence corresponds to the metal lead.

NIRGAL *see* NERGAL

NISABA—The *Sumerian* agricultural goddess of writing and scribes; replaced by the god NABU in the Mardukite *Babylonian* Anunnaki tradition.

NUDIMMUD *see* ENKI

NUNAMIR *see* ENLIL

NUSKU [*"Bringer of Light"*]—ENLIL's vizier.

NUZKU *see* NUSKU

OANNES *see* ENKI

RAMMAN(U) *see* ADAD

SAMAS {20}—The official solar deity of the Enlilite *Sumerian* Anunnaki pantheon, brother to IN-ANNA (SHTAR), born of NANNA and NINGAL. The sun represents the brilliance and radiant energy of life on earth; the light that allows organic life to grow and even the manner of which 'time' [and 'lifespan'] is divided. Expansive powerful energy of the solar current is invoked in magical ceremonies for general success and well-being. The fiery nature of the 'star' is called upon to 'incinerate iniquities' and reveal the nature of darkness and lies, meaning: the revelation of truth. Mistaken (by modern scholars) as monotheistic 'sun worship', solar veneration is really the celebration of life. As an archetypal representative of the 'starry' 'heavens', the sun signifies a presence and watchful eye of the 'All-Seeing-God', invoked in matters of law to bring righteous judgment. Sunday is sacred to SAMAS along with the color yellow, and both the color and essence of gold.

SARPANIT {(5)/(45)}—Seventh generation of ADAPA (by ENKI), the chosen royal spouse (consort) of MARDUK; princess-queen patron goddess (ISHTAR) of *Babylon* and mother to NABU. In alternative versions of the lore, her name ERU (or ERUA) designates her as the 'mother-goddess' of the '*Children of MARDUK*' (later associated with the light-folk or elves of Europe).

SHAMMASH *see* SAMAS

SHERIDA *see* AYA

SIN *see* NANNA

SUD *see* NINLIL

SUEN *see* NANNA

TAMMUZ *see* DUMUZI

TEHOM *see* TIAMAT

TIAMAT [*"Life-Giving Mother"*]—The 'primeval dragon' in *Babylonian* archaic epics, often equated with the *Sumerian* KUR. Later esoteric traditions associate 'her' as *Yaldabaoth* (*Ialda-baoth*) in Gnostic Hermeticism, or *Khornozon* (*Choronzon*) in Enochian Hermeticism. She is equated with the 'waters' or the 'Deep' in post-Sumerian Semitic scripture (Hebrew: *tehom*) – the all-encompassing "Sea" is parted to reveal the first 'division' (fragmentation) of "Life" in the Universe. She is paired anthropomorphically with ABZU (the *Abyss*) as the prehistoric 'ancestors' of the Anunnaki race. Her primary literary presence as TIAMAT (or T(I)AMTU) is in the *Enuma Elis* (*Babylonian*) 'Epic of Creation'. In later times, the name is used for the wife of ADAMU (*Adam*), being the equivalent to the Semitic "Eve" character.

TUTU *see* NABU

UDDU/UTTU *see* SAMAS

ZARPANITUM *see* SARPANIT

ANUNNAKI BIBLE

The Cuneiform Scriptures

New Standard Zuist Edition

an abridged version of
"*The Complete Anunnaki Bible*"
edited by Joshua Free
for founding the
Church of Mardukite Zuism
in hardcover and
pocket paperback

THE TABLETS OF DESTINY (REVELATION)

How Long-Lost Anunnaki Wisdom Can Change The Fate of Humanity

Mardukite Systemology Liber-One

based on the lectures
by Joshua Free for
Mardukite Academy

**THE
METAPHYSICS
OF STRANGER
THINGS**

*Telekinesis,
Telepathy &
Systemology*

by Joshua Free

in hardcover
and
paperback

**ANUNNAKI
TAROT**

*The Babylonian
Oracle
(Second Edition)*

Mardukite Liber-T

by Joshua Free

A guidebook featuring
the Archetypes of the
Major Arcana in
Ancient Mesopotamia.

First time in hardcover!

Collector's Edition Hardcover

THE FUNDAMENTALS OF
SYSTEMOLOGY

A Basic Course by
Joshua Free

*collecting material of six lesson-booklets
together in one volume!*

"Being More Than Human"

"Realities in Agreement"

"Windows To Experience"

"Ancient Systemology"

"A History of Systemology"

"Systemology Processing"

All *six* lesson-booklets of the first official
Basic Course on Mardukite Systemology
are combined together in *one volume* as
"Fundamentals of Systemology."

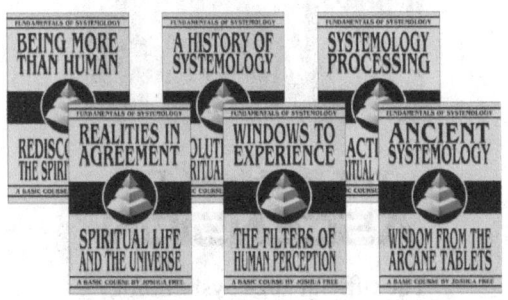

Lesson booklets are also available individually!

Collector's Edition Hardcover

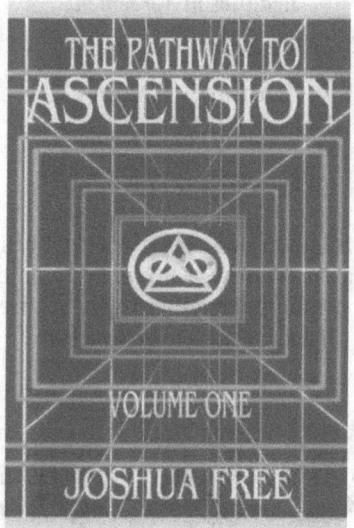

THE PATHWAY TO
ASCENSION

The Official 2024 Systemology
Professional Course by
Joshua Free

All sixteen lessons available in two volumes!

"Increasing Awareness"

"Thought & Emotion"

"Clear Communication"

"Handling Humanity"

"Free Your Spirit"

"Escaping Spirit-Traps"

"Eliminating Barriers"

"Conquest of Illusion"

All *sixteen* lesson-booklets of the newest
Professional Course on Mardukite Systemology
are combined together in *two volumes* as
"The Pathway to Ascension."

Lesson booklets are also available individually!

PUBLISHED BY THE **JOSHUA FREE** IMPRINT REPRESENTING

The Founding Church of Mardukite Zuism

THE JOSHUA FREE IMPRINT
JFI PUBLICATIONS

MARDUKITE
ZUISM

mardukite.com